INDEPENDENT LEARNING AND LITERACY

Related Titles

Teaching Oral Communication in Grades K–8
Ann L. Chaney and Tamara L. Burk
ISBN: 0-205-18938-5

Elementary Reading: Strategies That Work
Beth G. Davis and Bonnie Lass
ISBN: 0-205-15961-3

Assessment and Instruction of Culturally and Linguistically Diverse Students With or At-Risk of Learning Problems: From Research to Practice
Virginia Gonzalez, Rita Brusca-Vega, and Thomas Yawkey
ISBN: 0-205-15629-0

Developing Reading and Writing Through Author Awareness: Grades 4–8
Evelyn Krieger
ISBN: 0-205-17355-1

Developing Verbal Talent: Ideas and Strategies for Teachers of Elementary and Middle School Students
Joyce VanTassel-Baska, Dana T. Johnson, and Linda Neal Boyce
ISBN: 0-205-15945-1

INDEPENDENT LEARNING AND LITERACY

Strategies for Elementary Teachers

Patricia A. Genick
University of Michigan

Allyn and Bacon
Boston London Toronto Sydney Tokyo Singapore

Library of Congress Cataloging-in-Publication Data

Genick, Patricia A.
    Independent learning and literacy : strategies for
elementary teachers / Patricia A. Genick.
        p.   cm.
    Includes bibliographical references and index.
    ISBN 0-205-19806-6
    1. Independent study—United States.   2. Elementary education—
United States—Curricula.   3. Learning, Psychology of.
4. Metacognition in children—United States.   5. Classroom
management—United States.   I. Title.
    LB1601.3.G46   1997
    371.3´043—dc20   96-20925
                                                              CIP

LB1601.3
.G46
1997

Printed in the United States of America
10   9   8   7   6   5   4   3   2   1   00   99   98   97   96

I'd like to dedicate this book to my mother, Elsie M. Baker (now deceased) for her undying love, support, and encouragement throughout my life. And to my three sons Ray, Jeff, and Tom with all my love.

Contents

Chapter 3   Strategies in Reading/Writing   25

Chapter 4   Integrating the Curriculum   61

Chapter 5   Creating a Classroom Library   71

Chapter 6   Assessment (Making Sense of Standardized Tests and Using Authentic Tests)   97

Chapter 7   Designing Rubrics and Setting Criteria   114

Chapter 8   Celebrations of Learning, Portfolios, and Student-Led Conferencing   140

Chapter 9   Community Schools and Partnerships   156

Chapter 10   Demonstrating Learning Using Multimedia Techniques   177

Preface

Did you ever wonder if perhaps you were doing some everyday chores that could easily be performed by students? How about those papers you carry home at the end of the day? How about the endless hours of questions you answer every day? What about the various groups in which you preside that take most of your mornings and some afternoons? When do you find time to spend with individual children and to plan those extended lessons that reach all the students in your room? How can some of these endeavors be accomplished by students in an organized and structured way? How can we assess the learning that is taking place?

These questions have plagued me for the past ten years. So, in my capacity as a teacher, consultant, college instructor, and even parent, I set about to find the answers. Through observations, discussions, and teaching (all levels; K–12–College) I have composed my thoughts into what I hope will be a book to help those of you who would like to create independent learners.

Upon making a decision that I wanted to write a book about learning to learn, I read an article that helped me to focus on important issues (Wang, Haertel, & Walberg, 1993).[1] Research seemed to be confirming my feelings about independent learning. The studies that were conducted using 179 handbook chapters and reviews, 91 research syntheses, and surveying 61 educational researchers with a resulting knowledge base comprising 11,000 statistical findings not only confirmed what I believed but certainly coincided with the beliefs of many teachers with whom I have been in contact.

Briefly stated, the study concluded that direct influences rather than indirect made the most impact on learning; and, that there were six categories or broad types of influences:

1. Student Aptitude

2. Classroom Instruction and Climate

3. Context

4. Program Design

5. School Organization

6. State and District Characteristics

Student aptitude was the most influential of the six broad types of influences. Under student aptitude, these four areas were most significant:

1. Metacognitive Processes—A student's capacity to plan, monitor, and, if necessary, re-plan learning strategies.

2. Cognitive Processes—General intelligence, prior knowledge, competency in reading and mathematics, and verbal knowledge.

3. Social and Behavioral Attributes—Children who engage in constructive behaviors are more likely to perform well.

4. Motivational and Affective Attributes—Motivation determines effort and perseverance develops self-controlled and self-regulated learners.

Categories	Examples of One Variable in Category
Student Aptitude includes gender; academic history; and a variety of social, behavioral, motivational, cognitive, and affective characteristics.	
1. Metacognitive Processes	Comprehension monitoring (planning; monitoring effectiveness of attempted actions and outcomes of actions; testing, revising, and evaluating learning strategies)
2. Cognitive Processes	Level of specific academic knowledge in subject area
3. Social and Behavioral Attributes	Positive, nondisruptive behavior
4. Motivational and Affective Attributes	Attitude toward subject matter instructed
5. Psychomotor Skills	Psychomotor skills specific to area instructed
6. Student Demographics	Gender and socioeconomic status
Classroom Instruction and Climate includes classroom routines and practices, characteristics of instruction as delivered, classroom management, monitoring of student progress, quality and quantity of instruction provided, student-teacher interactions, and classroom atmosphere.	
7. Classroom Management	Group alerting (teacher uses question/ recitation strategies that maintain active participation by all students)
8. Student and Teacher Social Interactions	Positive student responses to questions from teacher and other students
9. Quantity of Instruction	Active engagement in learning
10. Classroom Climate	Cohesiveness (class members share common interests and values and emphasize cooperative goals)
11. Classroom Instruction	Clear and organized direct instruction
12. Academic Interactions	Frequent calls for substantive oral and written response

**TABLE P–1
Twenty-eight
Categories of
Influence on
School Learning**

(Cont.)

TABLE P–1 *(Cont.)*

Categories	*Examples of One Variable in Category*
13. Classroom Assessment	Assessment used as a frequent, integral component of instruction
14. Classroom Implementation and Support	Establishing efficient classroom routines and communicating rules and procedures

Context includes community demographics, peer culture, parental support and involvement, and amount of time students spend out of class on such activities as television viewing, leisure reading, and homework.

15. Home Environmental/Parental Support	Parental involvement in ensuring completion of homework
16. Peer Group	Level of peers' academic aspirations
17. Community Influences	Socioeconomic level of community
18. Out-of-Class Time	Student participation in clubs and extracurricular school activities

Problem Design refers to the physical and organizational arrangements for instructional delivery and includes strategies specified by the curriculum and characteristics of instructional materials.

19. Curriculum Design	Instructional materials employ advance organizers
20. Curriculum and Instruction	Alignment among goals, content, instructions, student assignments, and evaluation
21. Program Demographics	Size of instructional group (whole class, small group, one-on-one instruction)

School Organization refers to culure, climate, policies, and practices; includes demographics of the student body, whether the school is public or private, funding for categorical programs, school-level decision-making variables, and school-level policies and practices.

22. School Culture	Schoolwide emphasis on and recognition of academic achievement
23. Teacher/Administrator Decision Making	Principal actively concerned with instructional program
24. Parental Involvement Policy	Parental involvement in improvement and operation of instructional program
25. School Demographics	Size of school
26. School Policies	Explicit schoolwide discipline policy

State and District Characteristics refers to governance and administration, state curriculum and textbook policies, testing and graduation requirements, teacher licensure, provisions in teacher contracts, and district-level administrative and fiscal variables.

27. State-Level Policies	Teacher licensure requirements
28. District Demographics	State district size

Classroom Management	64.8
Metacognitive Processes	63.0
Cognitive Processes	61.3
Home Environment/Parental Support	58.4
Student/Teacher Social Interactions	56.7
Social/Behavioral Attributes	55.2
Motivational Affective Attributes	54.8
Peer Group	53.9
Quantity of Instruction	53.7
School Culture	53.3
Classroom Climate	52.3
Classroom Instruction	52.1
Curriculum Design	51.3
Academic Interactions	50.9
Classroom Assessment	50.4
Community Influences	49.0
Psychomotor Skills	48.9
Teacher/Administrator Decision Making	48.4
Curriculum and Instruction	47.7
Parental Involvement Policy	45.8
Classroom Implementation/Support	45.7
Student Demographics	44.8
Out-of-Class Time	44.3
Program Demographics	42.8
School Demographics	41.4
State-Level Policies	37.0
School Policies	36.5
District Demographics	32.9

TABLE P–2
Relative Influences on Learning

Types of Influence	Average Influence
Student Aptitude	54.7
Classroom Instruction and Climate	53.3
Context	51.4
Program Design	47.3
School Organization	45.1
State and District Characteristics	35.0

TABLE P–3
Average Percentages of Relative Influences

My book will discuss in detail the areas of most influence and will address activities and strategies to use in all the categories. It is organized in such a manner as to encourage you to help your students become independent and self-directed learners.

Let us begin by examining a classroom and the daily functions of its inhabitants. Let us see how we can create an independent classroom that is more student- than teacher-centered, where students feel safe and comfortable and where they will risk taking chances in order to learn. Let us see how they can be empowered by being given choices and where the atmosphere creates self-respect and self-reflection, where a mirror reflects creativity and self-appreciation and where all the students live like a family, assisting and respecting one another.

WHAT IS AN INDEPENDENT LEARNER?
• One who takes responsibility for his own actions. • One who sets and works toward goals. • One who assesses his own progress. • One who has a vision for himself or herself and creates alternatives.

ENDNOTE

1. Wang, Margaret C., Haertel, Geneva, and Walberg, Herbert. "What Helps Students Learn: Twenty-Eight Categories of Influence on School Learning." *Educational Leadership,* 51:4 (1993): pp. 74–79.

Acknowledgments

It is with heartfelt gratitude and appreciation that I thank the following people for making the job of writing this book easier. First, I'd like to thank the secretaries from the University of Michigan for their competent assistance and patience throughout this long endeavor. Trish, Beth, and Lisa—Thank you so very much!

Next I'd like to thank Shelly Potter for her writing of chapter 8, which discusses celebrations of independent learning, student-led conferencing, and portfolios. Her actual years of experience doing these things lent a reality to the writing that can only be done by first-hand knowledge. Thanks my friend!

One can only imagine how difficult it would be without those special members of your family and friends that support, encourage, and listen to your enthusiasm, excitement, and yes, complaints, frustrations, and impatience as you write a book. So, it is with great pleasure and appreciation that I list the following folks: My three sons—Jeff, who lives with me and who was closest to me during moments of great joy as I found the right words to express myself and also was cognizant of the hours of work (sometimes into the night), frustrations, and impatience when I couldn't seem to write anything at all. Next my thanks to Raymond and Tom who were there at times to lend an ear to my comments and occasionally listen to parts of the book. To my sister Joyce, who has shown such love and understanding through the years. And to my brother Chuck, whom I know I can always count on. To my in-laws Jean and John, who have always been more like sister and brother to me. Thank you for your constant love, caring, and sharing during all the times of joy. Though I lost my parents at an early age, I wish to thank them for teaching me to honor a good education and to appreciate the power of words, reading, and writing. They steadfastly encouraged me to pursue my dreams and to become whatever I chose to be. Last, but certainly not least, I'd like to thank Ray Sr. for his support and encouragement in the early years that allowed me to accomplish my goals (often by watching and caring for our sons for many long hours). To the rest of my family, Connie, Cathy, Debbie, Johnny, Barbie, Chuck and Bob, thank you as well for being such wonderful young, people that made us all proud.

After my family I need to recognize and thank my dearest friends, who are always there through good times and bad, sorrow and happiness, and have sustained me, when needed, while I was writing this book. Dee Allison, Doty Hodges, Sharie Kavanaugh, Shirley Michaels,

Marilyn Wilt, Ann Bolan, Pat Sestak, and Carole Gillan. I thank you all from the bottom of my heart for all your support and encouragement—I love you all!

I'd like to also recognize some people whom I believe are directly responsible for any success I've gained in the last few years. They have encouraged me to reach whatever goals I've set and to continue to grow as an educator. I want to thank Nancy Hawley, my dear friend, who is always there encouraging, advising, and lending a hand in whatever I do; Helen Burz, who was probably the first person to encourage me to contribute more to my profession, Sandy Schwartz, who was a constant friend and mentor, listening to my ideas, plans, and goals and encouraging me to reach beyond whatever I had decided to do, and Muriel, my long time friend, who was there at the beginning while I was trying to put my thoughts together and outline the book. Her suggestions helped me to focus on what I really wanted to say. Thanks to all of you for your inspiration and time, but most of all, thank you for always believing in me!

There are so many of my friends that went out of their way to get information for me or assist me in recalling and gathering materials that I'd like to thank: Shannon Ross, my friend who was encouraging and helpful and unrelenting in searching for reference items for me; Sue Ostrowski, Sue Reepmeyer, and Dale Truding, for providing me with, and giving permission to use the materials on the bank, the town of Midvale and the new school of choice—B.C.S.C. Thank you also to the Birmingham Public Schools for allowing me to use the literature concerning these projects and events and for encouraging me in my personal development as a professional educator. Kudos to all the wonderful staff members who went so far beyond their duties to respond to children's needs: Tom Zabawa, Liz Cunningham, Jane Klatt, Nancy Meyers, Nancy Straub, Ruth Goulding, Dolores Lane (the best secretary of all time), Betty Morris, and all the others at Midvale—a special thanks to you all!

Finally, I want to thank Virginia Lanigan, the senior editor at Allyn and Bacon, for her expert guidance, encouragement, and assistance in helping me to complete this project.

INDEPENDENT LEARNING
AND LITERACY

CHAPTER 1

Creating an Environment

PHILOSOPHY

The American Psychological Association Presidential Task Force on Psychology in Education has developed twelve learner-centered principles that I believe will help us decide on important visions and practices in our classrooms. These principles will continue to evolve, as research is ongoing. But they will give us a base from which to plan a classroom environment and its activities, strategies, and lessons. Each chapter will begin with one or more principles (APA Task Force on Psychology in Education, 1992).[1]

Before we begin discussing the principles guiding creating a classroom environment, I think we also need to consider the following beliefs. (Birmingham Public Schools, 1990).[2]

- The primary goal of education is the development of the whole person.

- All people can learn.

- Learning how to learn is a crucial skill.

- A positive self-image fosters effective learning.

- Effective learning helps students connect and apply information and ideas.

- People learn in different ways and in different contexts.

- Each person deserves to learn and work in a safe and accepting environment.

- Each person has intrinsic dignity and worth and deserves to be treated with respect.

- Expectations effect performance.

- Achievement requires commitment.

- We benefit from diversity.

LEARNING PRINCIPLES

This chapter addresses creating an environment and the following principles apply:

Principle 5—*Motivational Influences on Learning.* The depth and breadth of information processed, and what and how much is learned and remembered, is influenced by (a) self-awareness and beliefs about personal control, competence, and ability; (b) clarity and saliency of personal values, interests, and goals; (c) personal expectations for success or failure; (d) affect, emotion, and general states of mind; and (e) the resulting motivation to learn.

Principle 6—*Intrinsic Motivation to Learn.* Individuals are naturally curious and enjoy learning in the absence of intense negative cognitions and emotions (e.g., insecurity; worrying about failure; being self-conscious or shy; fearing corporal punishment or verbal ridiculing or stigmatizing labels).

There are four sayings that I have always thought guided my daily work in a classroom: two new ones and two old ones.

I hear, and I forget
I see, and I remember
I do, and I understand.
   — Chinese proverb

Tell a child what *to think and you make him a slave to* your *knowledge.*
Teach him how *to think and you make* all *knowledge his slave.*
     —Henry A. Taitt, 1982

You can teach a man (or woman) nothing. You can only help him (her) to discover it within himself (or herself).
     —Galileo

Students should not be expected to become independent learners independently.
     —Herber, 1987

Questions to be discussed:

I. How should I arrange my classroom to achieve maximum learning?

II. What are the steps to creating a comfortable risk-free atmosphere?

III. How can I develop self-esteem and self-direction in children with problems?

IV. How can I have a room that looks and feels student-centered and creative?

V. What are some skills for developing self-directed learning?

I. How should I arrange my classroom to achieve maximum learning?

Before your students arrive:

A. Put colorful paper up on all your boards and use borders to frame them. Do a board or two of your own if you want to make the room more reflective of your personality or philosophy. Some teachers are uncomfortable with a bare room and also enjoy being creative with their bulletin boards. This is purely a matter of choice.

B. Make special name tags for every child in your room. (Find out something about every child that is positive and can be written on each tag such as, always smiling, loves to write, enjoys reading, and so forth. Ask a former teacher, parent, and so on, for input.) If this seems too complicated or not possible or desirable to do, simply make colorful name tags that will appeal to the age of your youngsters. Children like to have something different than what they're used to, so be creative.

C. Arrange for, plan, and invite your students to a "before school starts" party the week before school begins or during the days before your youngsters return that you are at school preparing for the year ahead. The party can be for an hour or less. The important thing is to make your children feel comfortable with one another and eager to start the school year. So many children fear facing the unknowns of a new teacher, new classmates, or even a new school that in some cases we need to do whatever we can to ease that fear and welcome them back after the long summer hiatus. Here are some suggestions: change them, add to them, use your own creativeness, *but do something unique!*

1. Make the party simple, one to one-and-one-half-hours in duration. Serve something like popsicles, ice cream, popcorn, punch, and so forth.

2. Plan to get to know your students' names by using the special name tags and spending at least two to three minutes with each student.

3. Take pictures of your students at the party so that you can have a board of "beginnings" at your door or in the hall outside your classroom. It will help your students to feel comfortable and have something to talk about on the first day. Take candid shots of students talking together or have a child take some as you talk with groups of students.

4. Immediately after the party, enter in your observation journal your feelings and ideas about either individual students or the class as a whole. Make a list of interests that you heard expressed.

D. Have some simple activities planned such as relay races, telephone, and so on.

E. Arrange your desks or tables in groups of four. This will help contribute to a social climate where students help and support one another. Seat them randomly unless there are conflicts that arise, in which case you may have to change students' assignments. (See diagrams at the end of the chapter that you can try.)

II. What are the steps to creating a comfortable risk-free atmosphere?

A. Greet each student by name as they enter the classroom. (Have the name tags out in the hall and direct a student to be sure that the others put their tag on before going in.)

B. As soon as all students are seated, start "know your neighbor." Ask the students to talk with the person next to them for three minutes. At the end of that time, they need to tell the rest of the class at least two things that they learned about the person. (The teacher needs to also be a part of this procedure; someone should interview her/him and vice-versa.) If members are uneven, have one group be a threesome. For younger students they could tell just one thing about their neighbor.

C. Have students discuss next what a family is and how they live in harmony. Brainstorm by writing all suggestions on chart paper or on the board. Prioritize and categorize the suggestions explaining as you do this and enlisting their help. Categories that you might use are jobs, taking turns, respecting property, and so forth. Do not spend more than ten to fifteen minutes on this lesson. (This is a good time for lessons on why we prioritize and categorize. Make sure this is a mini-lesson and again make it short. You can always return to these topics of prioritizing/categorizing and should many times during the year.)

D. Create from these suggestions ways to live in harmony in this classroom, remembering to make rules simple and few in number. (It's easier to remember and follow a few simple rules.)

E. Do not suggest what will happen if the rules are broken. Instead, say how you know everyone will want to follow the rules and you expect you'll be so busy you won't even look at them as you'll be practicing them. (Usually if you catch students in the early stages of disobeying a rule, you can gently remind them of it and make no more of it than that. Students have a stake in the rules as they made them and you will see that they will help each other to follow them.) If they do break the rules and it is not possible to remind them quietly of their indiscretion, have the class decide what needs to be done or discipline that child and bring it up to the class later. It has always been my experience that schoolchildren just like your own will be more apt to push the limits of the rules if you make an issue of it. But you also always have a few that will do it anyway, no matter what you do. Get to know your children and do what you're most comfortable with doing. There are no hard and fast rules when it comes to behavior. I just know from experience that you usually get what you expect—if you expect the worst from your children, they will live up to your expectations and vice-versa.

F. The students' success in your classroom will depend in part on how well they communicate. So, from the first day on, your students need to understand communication. Brainstorm and write suggestions for what makes a good speaker and listener. *Note:* Remember that this is an ongoing activity that doesn't end with this discussion. In fact, developing effective communication skills needs to become an essential part of every day, modeled by the teacher and practiced by the students. How you communicate and respect your students' individuality is the key to their practicing that respect and caring for others. (At the end of this chapter, I will give you lists of behaviors and strategies for developing better speaking and listening skills as well as kinds of questions to ask to enhance this development.)

III. How can I develop self-esteem and self-direction in children with problems?

A. In the first week of school it is important to identify those students with special needs (either academically or emotionally). Usually in a classroom of twenty-five to thirty students you will find five or six children that need individual assistance. Then follow these steps:

1. Identify children with special needs experiencing problems.

2. When assigning jobs, explain that for the first two weeks you will pick the children for the jobs in the room.

3. Pick those children with special needs for those jobs.

4. Set up a schedule of meetings with your helpers (after school or lunch time).

5. Plan the sessions to get to know these children so that you and the class can help them.

6. Start modeling your acceptance and approval of these children. Remember, if you approve of them, so will your children. You will also allay discipline problems.

7. Set up a buddy system for assignments putting your students that need help with a stronger, accepting student that will support them. (Don't be afraid to change these buddies if they are incompatible.)

8. Be willing to modify individual assignments, if necessary, to accommodate those children experiencing academic difficulty, or to provide the extra help through parent aides or cross-age tutoring so that they can be successful. Make an appointment with a more experienced teacher or a special education teacher to help you plan how to do this or read teachers' journals, magazines, and books for ideas.

B. Begin in the first weeks of school to develop a system of support in your classroom. Follow these steps:

1. Send out a simple questionnaire asking for parent support.

2. Set up a meeting with the volunteers to discuss:

   a. hours needed for support.

   b. what you expect them to do (be specific).

   c. your philosophy and methods.

3. Arrange with teachers two years above your grade level to have students for support for your children.

4. Do not have the brightest children in these classes come in to support your youngsters. Choose average students with strong empathy for others.

5. Set up a meeting with these youngsters. Discuss:

   a. hours you need help.

   b. what you need them to do (be specific).

   c. your philosophy and methods.

C. Start setting up individual conference times for your children. As the year goes on and your students are more self-directed there will be more time available. Do the following:

1. Make a weekly schedule of possible times for conferences (approximately three to five minutes per child to start).

2. Begin with some of the children with problems (be sure to include a few others also).

3. Set up specific things you will do in these conferences remembering in the beginning that you will only meet for three to five minutes.

4. Organize these conferences around your helpers in some cases (you do not want your helpers to always be doing things with the whole class).

D. Set up a board in your room or on your door to record positive actions in your room. Steps to follow:

1. Identify a spot in your room where you can keep a daily record of good deeds.

2. Explain to your children what you are doing—model it.

3. Put such things on the board as, "John helped Jerry with his math today." . . . "Barbara learned how to multiply today." . . . "Patty gave up her turn for Mary." . . . "Bill always is willing to help others."

4. Do not keep the board up forever. Remember, your goal is to start focusing on positive actions in your room. (It becomes old after a few weeks.)

5. After you take it down, talk to your youngsters about an idea they might have to keep a positive feeling in your room. (Maybe helping others in the school and discussing those good deeds or perhaps helping at home, and so forth.)

IV. How can I have a room that looks and feels student-centered and creative?

A. Part of the agenda for the first day needs to include task assignments. It is very beneficial to have plants and animals in the room to encourage individual responsibility through their care. However, other jobs are also necessary to create a feeling of ownership in the classroom. You need to develop a list of those tasks and how to perform them.

B. You need to discuss how to develop a theme and what suggestions the students might have for the theme. It's important to set a purpose for learning immediately. (This will be discussed further in Chapter 4.)

C. Part of making your room child-centered has to do with how many things in the room are designed and produced by children. Therefore, it is crucial to start at the beginning of the year (preferably the first day) to begin filling the walls and room with their authentic work. You will need to assign some students to organize boards and to meet to plan this endeavor or, if the students are too young, to meet with a group yourself to begin this process. The rest of the students can be doing self-directed reading or a quiet activity at their tables.

D. It is important that first day or two to establish some type of communication system between teacher and student and student to student such as mailboxes, baskets for work, portfolio folders, work-in-process folders, and so on. Have your students plan with your guidance how this will work. It needs to be both practical and simple to use.

V. What are some skills for developing self-directed learning?

Have students practice these skills daily (model for them).

- Predicting

- Observing

- Comparing

- Estimating

- Inferring

- Drawing conclusions

- Measuring

- Classifying

- Reflecting

TABLE 1–1
Additional Ideas
and Activities
for Creating
a Friendly,
Comfortable
Classroom

1. Being a Friend
   Talk about what it means to be a friend.
   List ideas on the board.
   Discuss ways you can be a friend in the classroom.

2. Secret Pals
   Pick names from a basket each day.
   Do something special each day for that person.
   Share with your classmates, at the end of the week, all the nice things
      you did.

3. Friends in Other Classes
   Choose a person in another room (could be a reading buddy or a neighbor).
   Plan to do something nice for them such as write them a letter, smile
      at them in the hall, make a card for their birthday, give them a com-
      pliment, etc.

4. Read/Write to an Adult
   Choose an adult in the building (another teacher, the principal, custodian,
      an aide, etc.).
   Read a story to them or write them a card or letter.

5. Read Books, Poems
   Pick out books, poems, articles, pictures, etc., on friendship to read or share
      with your students each week.,
   Have students look for books, poems, articles to read aloud to the class.
   Share old greeting cards on friendship; read from them.
   Let students create their own cards to give to others.

TABLE 1–2   Communication and Listening Skills

When We Communicate We Need to:	*When We Listen We Need to:*
Be sure the persons to whom we speak can ask questions for clarification.	Ask questions when things are unclear.
Be sure not to filter out critical or opposite side views on the subject.	Disagree in a civil manner if necessary.
Be careful not to turn off listeners by giving sarcastic or flippant answers to questions.	Listen carefully and not interrupt.
Not belittle or give no credence to listeners' feelings or responses.	Not give generalizations like "Oh, that's not new—I already heard that," or "Everybody knows that."
	Not deny a person's feelings by saying, "Everyone feels like that sometimes," or "Everyone has those kinds of problems."

**TABLE 1–3
Poor Listeners**

1. "Tune out" the other person at the beginning of the conversation and determine what they're going to say before fully listening.
2. Think about a response while the other person is talking.
3. Are quick to find fault with speakers' grammar, skills, dialect, etc., instead of concentrating on content.
4. Pretend to be listening.
5. Only listen to part of what the other person is saying and take notes only on that part.
6. Distract the speaker by talking or otherwise doing something else.
7. Only listen when it's easy to understand; stop listening when it becomes harder.
8. Become emotional over content and stop listening.
9. Write too much, listen too little.
10. Daydream about something mentioned, get totally off track.

**TABLE 1–4
Good Listeners**

1. Defer judgment, are more controlled.
2. Listen to the other person's complete thought before thinking about a response.
3. Do not allow grammar, dialect, or other speaking characteristics to interfere with content.
4. Listen carefully and are aware of becoming inattentive; work at staying alert.
5. Do not attempt to write while person is making a point; listen for main ideas.
6. Don't talk or otherwise create a distraction.
7. Clarify anything not understood by asking questions (if allowed), otherwise write down questions.
8. Do not allow emotions to interfere with listening.
9. Keep on track by focusing on points being made; avoid getting off the subject.
10. Don't worry about committing everything said to memory.

FIGURE 1–1 Student-Centered Classroom Arrangement One

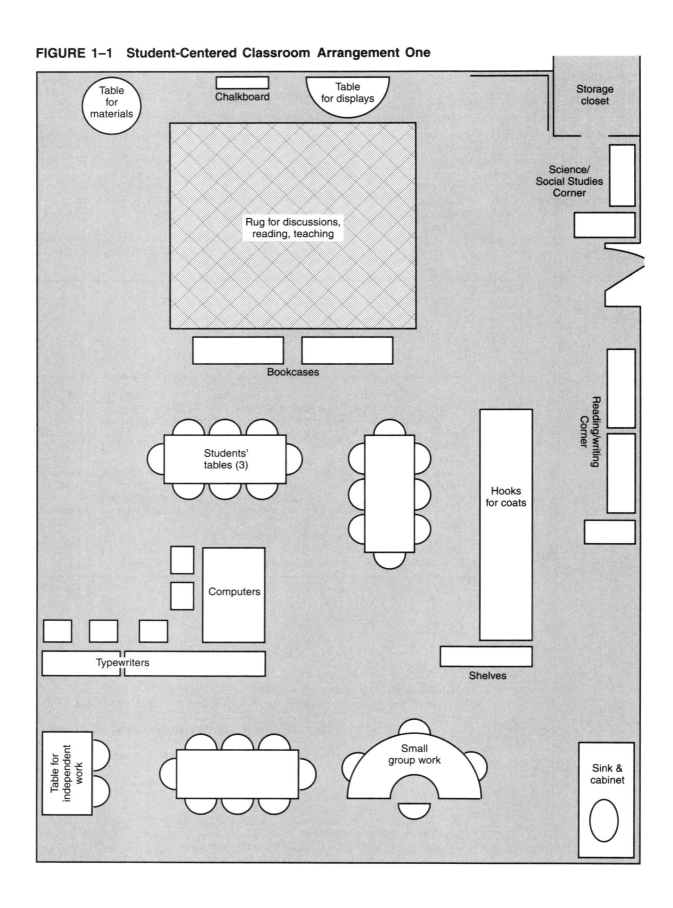

FIGURE 1–2 Student-Centered Classroom Arrangement Two

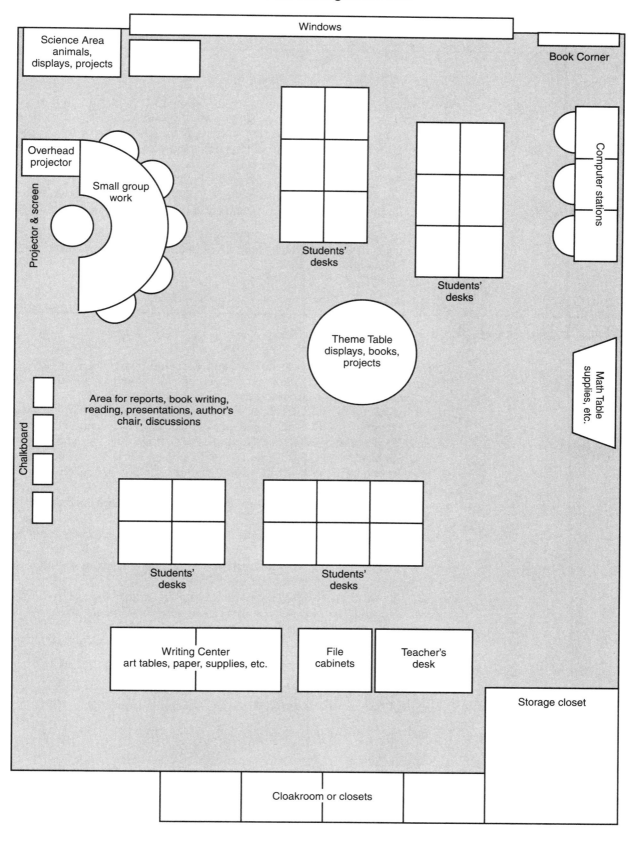

ENDNOTES

1. American Psychological Association Task Force on Psychology in Education. Draft. "Learner-Centered Psychological Principles— Guidelines for School Redesign and Reform." (August, 1992). Copyright © 1992 by the American Psychological Association. Reproduced with permission. This material presents a *working* draft report of the APA Presidential Task Force on Psychology in Education. This does *not* represent a statement of APA policy. Further reproduction without the express written permission of the APA is prohibited.

2. Birmingham Public Schools, Birmingham, Michigan. "Report to Board of Education by Committee on Developmentally Appropriate Practices." November 28, 1990.

REFERENCES

American Psychological Association Task Force on Psychology in Education. Draft. "Learner-Centered Psychological Principles—Guidelines for School Redesign and Reform." (August, 1992).

Copyright © 1992 by the American Psychological Association. Reproduced with permission. This material presents a *working* draft report of the APA Presidential Task Force on Psychology in Education. This does *not* represent a statement of APA policy. Further reproduction without the express written permission of the APA is prohibited.

Birmingham Public Schools, Birmingham, Michigan. "Report to Board of Education by Committee on Developmentally Appropriate Practices." (November 28, 1990).

Green, Pamela, and Furnise, Elaine. *The Literary Agenda: Issues for the Nineties.* Portsmouth, NH: Heinemann, 1991, pp. 17–34.

Herber, Harold L., and Nelson-Herber, Joan. "Developing Independent Learners," *Journal of Reading* 1987.

Pappas, Christine C.; Kiefer, Barbara Z.; and Levstik, Linda S. *An Integrated Language Perspective in the Elementary School: Theory into Action.* White Plains, NY: Longman, pp. 326–338.

Routman, Regie. *Invitations: Changing as Teachers and Learners K–12.* Toronto, Canada: Irwin; Portsmouth, NH: Heinemann, 1991, pp. 419–457.

Taitt, Henry A. *TLC for Growing Minds. Microcomputer Projects. Advanced Projects for Adults.* Creative Learning Association, 1983.

Cooperative Groups

PHILOSOPHY

In today's world it is essential that we learn to live in harmony, accepting each other and working as a team with others to solve problems whether they be at work, at home, or in the community. By learning to work together, we will also appreciate the skills and unique talents of individuals and help them to reach their potential. We must never lose sight of the fact that we need to develop leaders that are strong in their beliefs and able to function well on their own independently.

If we teach children to work together for a common purpose in schools, we will certainly encourage that behavior in their lives outside of school as well. Chapter 2 is devoted to assisting you in establishing varied types of groups that will lead to independence, creativity, and cooperativeness in your students.

LEARNING PRINCIPLES

This chapter addresses cooperative groups and the following principles apply:

Principle 9—*Social and Cultural Diversity*. Learning is facilitated by social interactions and communication with others in a variety of flexible, diverse (cross-age, culture, family background, and so on), and adaptive instructional settings.

Principle 10—*Social Acceptance, Self-Esteem, and Learning*. Learning and self-esteem are heightened when individuals are in respectful and caring relationships with others who see their potential, genuinely appreciate their unique talents, and accept them as individuals.

Questions to be discussed:

I. What are cooperative groups and why should I use them?

II. How do I organize these groups?

III. How can I use this organization in practice?

IV. How can the room be arranged?

V. What is interdependency and how do I teach it?

VI. What are the various groupings I can use?

VII. How do I assess and evaluate the learning taking place?

VIII. What are the steps to follow when establishing (1) criteria for grading, (2) peer evaluation, and (3) individual evaluations?

IX. How do I evaluate a small group's performance?

X. How do I keep track of student learning?

XI. How do I get started?

XII. What are some things to remember and consider?

I. What are cooperative groups and why should I use them?

"Cooperate," according to the *American College Dictionary* means "to work or act together or jointly; unite in producing an effect."[1]

There is also an old saying, "Two heads are better than one." We should consider the benefits of this concept in the classroom. Children who are truly working together on a project or assignment can gather more information and debate its relevance more thoroughly than by working alone. Students need to share with and support one another. They can challenge and encourage academic excellence.

The concept of working together in a team is very popular in industry today and business leaders are asking educators to help them by exposing students to more group work. By learning how to encourage students to use their individual talent and skills to assist the group, we are letting students model this expertise for others. We are also exposing children to many ways of looking at and solving problems.

Socrates, Plato, and all the ancient philosophers shared ideas, concepts, and planned together how to solve problems. Socialization is a vital part of our nature and if group work is planned carefully, all students benefit.

William Glasser, in an interview by Gough (1987) discusses special groupings in band, music, and so forth, and how they work well. He suggests that teachers try the same kind of grouping in classrooms that work in extracurricular activities.

The most definitive work in research having to do with cooperative grouping comes from David and Roger Johnson (1984).[2] They have trained thousands of teachers to incorporate cooperative learning into their classrooms. They have conducted more than eighty original studies and have concluded that children who learn cooperatively compared with those who learn competitively or independently learn better, feel better about themselves, and get along better with each other. They suggest, as well, five simple steps for teaching cooperation (Johnson and Johnson, 1987).[3]

II. How do I organize these groups?

In determining the use of various random groups on achievement, one must look at research to see whether groupings of any particular kind are important for learning.

For years researchers have been studying homogeneous ability) versus heterogeneous (random) groupings in a classroom. In the early 1920s and 1930s, authors listed advantages and disadvantages of homogeneous or ability groupings.

---

1. *Help students become aware of the need for each skill.* The types of interaction possible in a classroom are cooperation, competition, and independent work. Anything that is done individually within the group is just one part of the whole that the team must produce.

2. *Help students gain a clear understanding of each skill.* Cooperation depends on accepting others' opinions (not necessarily agreeing with them) and on listening without criticism or interruption.

3. *Give students situations in which they can practice social skills.* These do not have to be related to a particular lesson or even a specific content area. For example, the situations could include computing the average distance between the students' homes and the school or listing the names of students' favorite musicians. The teacher should move from group to group acting as a facilitator, posing questions and statements intended to help students solve the problem on their own and use the necessary skills.

4. *Give all students feedback on their performance of the skill.* The teacher or an appointed student monitor observes the team in action and gives factual information, such as "Alex asked four questions" or "Zak summarized and clarified statements three times." An observer should not classify the responses as good or bad. Students can use forms to record responses, and then, at the end of the session, each student can evaluate how well the team worked together. Feedback is a vital component of successful collaborative teamwork.

5. *Persevere in practicing the skill.* Teachers and students must be prepared for problems and difficulties when beginning collaborative learning. They will encounter a change in the teacher/student role, a power shift from teacher to students, and questions about teachers' own responsibilities. Teachers will find themselves asking, "Can I trust students to work together? Will the better students do all the work? Will the team turn into just a social group? Will students go home and complain to their parents that I am not teaching them anything?"

**TABLE 2–1
Johnson and
Johnson's Five
Simple Steps for
Group Cooperation**

Source: Johnson, D., and Johnson, R. *Learning Together and Alone: Cooperative, Competitive, and Individualistic Learning.* 2nd ed. (Englewood Cliffs, NJ: Prentice Hall, 1987).

A. Advantages of ability grouping:

1. It permits pupils to make progress commensurate with their abilities.

2. It makes possible an adaptation of the technique of instruction to the needs of the group.

3. It reduces failure.

4. It helps maintain interest and incentive because bright students are not bored by participation of the less bright.

5. Slower students participate more when not eclipsed by those much brighter.

6. It makes possible individual instruction to small, slow groups.

B. Disadvantages of ability grouping:

1. Slow pupils need the presence of able students to stimulate and encourage them.

2. A stigma is attached to low groups that discourages pupils in these groups from trying to do their best work.

3. Teachers are unable or do not have time to differentiate the work for different levels of ability.

4. Teachers object to slower groups.

These ideas have not changed very much since this study, however, we are learning more about the idea of grouping. The real issue in developing an instructional model is not whether we should group full-time, flexible, within class, across grades, or no groups. Grouping alone doesn't ensure academic achievement. It is the careful modifications such as reinforcement, remediation, and enrichment that determine the students' achievement. The most important value of flexible grouping by achievement is the enhancement of the delivery of appropriate instruction leading to success for all students.

Teachers must not form expectations based on IQ scores. The idea that human ability is fixed at an early age and that achievement differences in school are due to these abilities has been challenged by the evidence that ability is developmental. Cognitive psychologists provide evidence that abilities can be learned. (It would be wise to read as much as you can about learning styles of children in the journals. I've included the names of many in Chapter 5.)

Research leaves us with a paradox: not all types of grouping are good for all students. Many educators express concern that we are concentrating too much on students' abilities to work together and not enough on individual achievement. Industry is promoting the idea that we need to teach children to work together as a team to solve problems. In attempting to satisfy that request, we are sometimes forgetting to consider the individual student as well. I believe it is possible to do both. In many situations, it is best to use a group approach, but in other instances we must allow individuals to demonstrate their ability to perform tasks and show they understand concepts and have the necessary basic skills to do their work.

The main issue in grouping students will be:

1. Who makes the decision and on what basis?

2. Are the groupings instructional or administrative?

3. Are they flexible and variable?

4. Are they continually evaluated as to their success?

If we were to examine all the different current research regarding grouping, we would find some of the same conclusions. However, the one change of which we are cognizant today is the impact of the affective domain. We know that self-esteem, confidence in oneself and one's ability to learn, determines motivation for learning regardless of ability (see Preface endnote for Wang, Haertel, Walberg, 1993).

So, it is important not only to randomly select the participants in grouping in a classroom for many tasks and assignments, but to also recognize the abilities of your students and group them in a more homogeneous manner for certain skill practice, reading to each other, and perhaps reflections on a particular story. It is important also that the assignments are differentiated when a child will be working independently.

Groupings should be varied and never used in exactly the same way over time. It is also necessary for students to work on their own at times to show mastery of skills and concepts.

Quizzes should be given at times to these students to determine what small groups could be formed that need practice on particular skills and direction by the teacher. (These skills can be discussed by the teacher and student during conference time as well. See Chapter 9.)

III. How can I use this organization in practice?

A. It is important to consider the following points when establishing any type of grouping. Do these things before grouping your students:

1. The groups should be no larger than three or four (you will have less talking and visiting).

2. Every person should have an assigned job (reader, reporter, checker, researcher, and so forth).

3. You need to discuss and establish rules for the group before they start. Be sure they use their own words. (You can always guide the selections of rules and add one or two of your own.)

4. Set up a purpose and a method(s) of reporting their progress. The assignment must be clearly understood by the students before they begin work.

5. Model group behavior by having role-playing of particular types of groups:

   a. Pick students.

   b. Assign them jobs in the group.

   c. Remind them of rules.

   d. Give them the assignment and guide behavior as the rest of the class observes their work.

(Pick a type of group from the list that follows and model several types of groups.)

IV. How can the room be arranged?

It's important to think ahead of time about how you will arrange your room during cooperative learning. You need to allow your students choices in seating, but also keep in mind that the students need to be compatible to work together. So let them have some choice, but don't hesitate to change groups the minute the group is not being productive.

V. What is interdependency and how do I teach it?

Teachers need to expect a single product from a group to promote the idea that collaborative learning does not mean that learning takes place in a totally relaxed, non-evaluative atmosphere. A team grade might be given to reinforce the idea that everyone is responsible for everyone else in the team. It fosters interdependency.

There is a difference in behavior by students not taught interdependence. Students need to learn and practice how to express ideas of their own and also respect the opinions of others. They need to learn how to support others, bridge and summarize information, and rephrase what they read and write.

VI. What are the various groupings I can use?

Keep in mind that these groupings may not be applicable to all grade levels. You will need to modify or alter the ideas to suit your particular situation.

A. Turn to your neighbor—Three to five minutes. Ask the students to turn to a neighbor and ask her/him something about the lesson; to explain a concept you have just taught; to explain the assignment; to explain how to do what you have just taught; to summarize the three most important points of the discussion; or whatever fits the lesson.

B. Reading Groups—Students read material together and answer the questions. One person is the Reader, another the Recorder, and the third the Checker (who checks to make certain everyone understands and agrees with the answers). They must come up with three possible answers to each question and circle their favorite one. When finished, they sign the paper to certify that they understand and agree on the answers.

C. Jigsaw—Each person reads and studies a part of a selection, then teaches what he or she has learned to the other members of the group. Each then quizzes the group members until satisfied that everyone knows his or her part thoroughly.

D. Focus Trios—Before a film, lecture, or reading, have students summarize together what they already know about the subject and come up with questions they have about it. Afterwards, the trios answer questions, discuss new information, and formulate new questions.

E. Reading Buddies—Have students read stories to each other, getting help with words, and discussing content with their partners; or, have students tell about their books and read favorite parts to each other.

F. Homework Checkers—Have students compare homework answers, discuss any they have not answered similarly, then correct their papers and add the reason they changed an answer. They make sure everyone's answers agree, then staple the papers together. You grade only one paper from each group and give members that grade.

G. Writing Response Groups—Students read and respond to each other's papers three times.

1. They mark what they like with a star and put a question mark anywhere they think something is weak or unclear. They then discuss the paper with the writer.

2. They mark problems with grammar usage, punctuation, spelling, or format and discuss it with the author.

3. They proofread the final draft and point out any errors for the writer to correct.

Note: Teachers can guide this procedure by assigning questions for students to answer about their group members' papers to help them focus on certain problems or skills.

H. Group Reports—Students research a topic together. Each one is responsible for checking at least one different source and writing at least three notecards of information. They write the report together; each person is responsible for seeing that his/her information is included. For oral reports, each must take a part and help each other rehearse until they are all at ease.

I. Playwrights—Students write a play or skit together (perhaps about a time period recently studied) then practice and perform it for the class.

J. Publishing Stories—Have groups work together to make covers for creative stories. Have a center where each group can work together to do this.

K. Math Groups—Have students work together on math assignments by using manipulatives, estimating answers, working problems, describing processes, and reporting to the rest of the class.

L. Science Groups—When reading an assignment or doing an experiment, be sure students have practice in small groups going through the steps of scientific inquiry of: (1) curriculum questioning, (2) predicting, (3) observing, (4) measuring, (5) classifying, (6) comparing, (7) making inferences, and (8) drawing conclusions (adapted from Johnson & Johnson, 1984).

VII. How do I assess and evaluate the learning taking place?

Once students are accustomed to working in a group, you can begin to observe the learning taking place. (Always give time for students to get comfortable with group work before evaluating.) You will need to assess the learning in two ways:

1. What is the quality of the group work?

2. How does the individual work compare to the quality of the group? Is the student working to his/her potential?

It is important to consider the following points when evaluating group work:

A. You must establish the criteria for grading.

B. You need to set up the criteria and then model it for the students.

C. After you set up the criteria, you need to ask the students for their ideas or the criteria they consider important and why.

VIII. What are the steps to follow when establishing (1) criteria for grading, (2) peer evaluation, and (3) individual evaluations?

A. Tell the class what the criteria for grading will be. (For younger children you need to keep it simple and add to the criteria as time progresses.)

B. Ask for additional criteria from the class.

C. Model the criteria by explaining in detail what you expect.

D. Write a whole class report, utilizing and clarifying the criteria again as you work together. (You may need to write more than one report together to help students understand.)

E. Use chart paper for the report(s) so that students can check later for important points of organization, purpose, and so on, and how you constructed the report.

F. List important points on a poster board to put up in your room for guidance. (Remember to explain that this learning is on-going.) You may change criteria as you go along, adding or deleting, as necessary.

Peer evaluation
Members of the group need to evaluate one another. As students become more used to being independent and learn how to work collaboratively, they will become more introspective about the learning of individuals. It is important to work with students to develop the criteria for this kind of evaluation so that students don't resent the evaluations.

First and foremost the students themselves need to develop the criteria. The following one is a guide and can be used to start developing your own criteria.

Individual work

The second area to consider when evaluating is the quality of the individual work. This is best done on a daily or weekly manner by having individual quizzes to determine understanding of the concepts or skills being taught whether it be in reading, writing, math, science, or social studies. Some teachers consider an essay-form quiz just asking what they have learned to suffice.

If a teacher is clear about what she or he is teaching and knows what outcomes are desired, the form of the assessment is not important. A good form to use when evaluating is the cloze technique. Cloze refers to the reading clozure practice required when readers fill in the blanks left in text using whatever knowledge and experience they have. They are valuable in evaluating reading ability and appropriateness of text.

IX. How do I evaluate a small group's performance?

A good way to evaluate small group performance is to again use a cloze test. Simply put, a cloze test consists of writing a paragraph on something you are studying and leaving blanks for some key concepts. The students then have to fill in the correct words that fit and make sense. In the early grades children can orally fill in the blanks as the teacher reads aloud a favorite story, big book, or predictable book the class has read together. Students can work in cooperative groups performing these tasks and challenging answers. There are many types of cloze tests you can make and trying one or two helps you create another kind for the group to try. (Check references listed at the end of the chapter.)

	5	4	3	2	1	0
Date						
1. I contributed my ideas and information.						
2. I asked others for their ideas and information.						
3. I summarized all our ideas and information.						
4. I shared my materials.						
5. I asked for help when I needed it.						
6. I helped the other members of my group learn.						
7. I made sure everyone in my group understood how to do the schoolwork we were assigned.						
8. I helped keep the group studying.						
9. I included everyone in our work.						

TABLE 2–2
As a Member
of a Group
How Am I doing?

X. How do I keep track of student learning?

We will be discussing portfolios and criteria and rubrics in the following chapters. Remember that you need to have students eventually determine their own criteria and scoring forms (with your guidance).

Another way that teachers keep track of learning is simply through observation. When your groups begin functioning on their own, it leaves time for you to circulate and start keeping anecdotal notes on individual students. These can then be read and assessed in conjunction with the quizzes you give, in a student/teacher conference time.

The most important thing to guard against is pigeonholing students and not continuing to impartially evaluate their work. It is an ongoing, never ending process and you must have high expectations for each and every one of your students and let them know this.

Another interesting way to determine whether your students are learning in group settings is to use data charts. The data chart usually addresses the content in a unit of work being done. It could come from science, health, or social studies. The materials used may be books, films or filmstrips, videos, magazines, newspapers, guest speakers, field trips, and so on.

XI. How do I get started?

A. Before starting to use group work, be sure you understand the concepts and principles of cooperative grouping. Remember to:

1. Use cooperative groups on a daily basis so children get used to working together.

2. Continuously evaluate the group work.

3. Look for new and different ways for students to work together to develop themes.

4. Eventually serve as coach or mentor, but be sure you do not allow children to work on their own until they show you they can and remember some children may not be ready yet to work on their own. Remember, too, that you are the one in charge throughout the year. There are many concepts you need to teach your children.

5. Assist students in locating resources and conducting research.

6. Expect noise. Busy students are active and need to reflect on their learning.

7. Observe behavior and be ready to re-evaluate groupings. Listen and sit in on groups to determine progress.

8. Expect good work and know that learning is continuous and you must keep students learning and motivated by challenging them with new ideas, concepts, and activities.

XII. What are some things to remember and consider?

1. Do I stress *how* to think rather than *what* to think?

2. Do students know and understand that sometimes there are many answers to questions rather than just one right answer?

3. When a child asks a question, do I say, "What do you think?"

4. Do I give reasons for giving a point of view?

5. Do I frequently model reading, writing, and thinking out loud?

6. Do I ask open-ended questions that require more than a short, one-syllable answer?

7. Do students engage in critiquing each other's work in thinking, reading, and writing?

8. Do I encourage students to relate their learning to their personal lives and to apply it to other subject matter?

9. Do students set purposes and objectives for their own learning after being taught to do so?

10. Do students collaborate at times to solve problems?

11. Do I make sure I stress individual understanding and achievement as well as group understanding?

12. Do I often allow students to continue in a worthwhile discussion of something rather than moving on to "cover" content?

13. Do I insist that students actively listen to each other's point of view?

14. Do I teach and model good manners and respect for one another?

15. Do I have a classroom atmosphere where students can take risks without fear of censure?

ENDNOTES

1. Clarence L. Barnhart, *The American College Dictionary*. New York: Random House, 1953, p. 267.

2. D. Johnson, and Johnson, R. *Circles of Learning: Cooperation in the Classroom*. Alexandria, VA: Association for Supervision and Curriculum Development, 1984.

3. D. Johnson, and Johnson, R. *Learning Together and Alone: Cooperative, Competitive, and Individualistic Learning*. 2nd ed. Englewood Cliffs, NJ: Prentice Hall, 1987.

REFERENCES

Barnhart, Clarence L. *The American College Dictionary*. New York: Random House, 1953, p. 267.

Elley, Warrick. *A Close Look at the Cloze Test*. Special Issue. New Zealand Council of Educational Research, n.d., 1980s.

Gough, P. B. "The Key to Improving Schools: An Interview with William Glasser." *Phi Delta Kappan* (1987): pp. 656–662.

Hornsby, David; Parry, Joann; and Sukarna, Deborah. "Data Charts" from *Teach On*. Portsmouth, NH: Heinemann, 1992, pp. 22–23.

Johnson, D., and Johnson, R. *Learning Together and Alone: Cooperative, Competitive, and Individualistic Learning*. 2nd ed. Englewood Cliffs, NJ: Prentice Hall, 1987.

Johnson, D., and Johnson, R. *Circles of Learning: Cooperation in the Classroom*. Alexandria, VA: Association for Supervision and Curriculum Development, 1984.

Leu, Donald, J., and Kinzer, Charles K. *Effective Reading Instruction K–8*. 2nd ed. New York: Macmillan, 1991, pp. 531–562.

Routman, Regie. Invitations: *Changing as Teacher and Learners K–12*. Toronto, Canada: Irwin; Portsmouth, NH: Heinemann, 1991, pp. 70–77.

Strategies in Reading/Writing

PHILOSOPHY

We know from practice that reading makes us better writers and writing makes us better readers, so it is important when considering strategies that we remember this connection. We also know that students learn better when they understand their own style of learning. It is important to help them become metacognitive (know how they learn) from the beginning of the year.

Chapter 3, therefore, will discuss various strategies that will enhance reading and writing. They will assist students in making connections to real life situations and challenge them to use metacognition.

LEARNING PRINCIPLES

This chapter will follow the principles of learning listed below:

Principle 3—*The Construction of Knowledge.* The learner organizes information in ways that associate and link new information with existing knowledge in uniquely meaningful ways.

Principle 4—*Higher-Order Thinking.* Higher-order strategies for "thinking about thinking"—for overseeing and monitoring mental operations—facilitate creative and critical thinking and the development of expertise.

Chapter 3 addresses these questions:

I. What is metacognition and how does it help students become self-directed learners?

II. What is meant by a system for learning in reading and writing?

III. What are the researched, tried, and true strategies that really work in developing better readers and writers?

IV. How can I help create a feeling in my students that they are readers and writers?

V. What role does phonics play in developing readers and writers?

VI. What are some activities and ideas for reading and writing in the classroom?

I. What is metacognition and how does it help students become self-directed learners?

A. Metacognition is a key for independent learning from text. When students learn to understand their own cognitive process or become metacognitive, they are better able to control or regulate their own learning. Within a classroom you have two types of students:

1. Those who, on their own, will reread something not clear, raise questions to clarify a point, and flexibly use reading as a tool for learning. They will also read for pleasure and will have learned how to use research or several sources of information in which to examine a topic or subject.

2. The other type of student never rereads, has little or no awareness of an occasional lack of understanding, does not realize how important it is to understand directions, and hasn't been able to use reading flexibly in the learning process. The difference in the two types of students may not be, as has been presumed, a disparity in their general learning ability background experiences, world knowledge, word recognition skills, vocabulary development or basic motivation to succeed. Indeed, many of these same students are found to perform as well as the prior type of student on reading tasks under direct supervision of the teacher.

   What may be occurring is the first student is displaying the knowledge of and ability to regulate his/her reading using strategies that suit his/her personality or learning style or is, what we call, metacognitive. The second student is not systematically using suitable strategies in order to learn (Babbs, Moe, 1983).[1] One strategy that is prevalent in the research today that addresses metacognition is reciprocal teaching (Palincsar, Ransom, 1988),[2] which was devised to facilitate a group effort between teacher and students in bringing meaning to text. The particular strategies used are:

    a. Summarizing—identifying, paraphrasing, and integrating the most important information in the text.

    b. Question Generating—identifying the kind of information that is important enough to warrant a question, then passing the information in question form and self-testing to see if they can answer it.

    c. Clarifying—attention is called to the fact that there may be many reasons why text is difficult to understand. They are taught to be alert to such impediments and to take steps to restore meaning.

    d. Predicting—hypothesizing what the author will discuss next in the text using clues and prior or background knowledge they already possess.

B. Introducing the procedure: how does it help students become self-directed learners?

    1. Discuss with the students why text may be difficult to understand (give examples of hard text), why it is important to use strategies (give examples of strategies you use), and how reciprocal teaching will help.

    2. You will need to go over each strategy describing it and the reason for learning it. (Summarizing, Question Generating, Clarifying, Predicting)

    3. Begin a dialogue about something you've read modeling the strategies, perhaps using some bright, motivated students to answer and also serve as models and motivators. However, all students should participate noting at least one fact they recall.

    4. After many dialogues where the teacher models and instructs the students, it is important to consciously try to impart responsibility for the dialogue to the students. You will then assume the role of coach and provide evaluation to the pupils regarding their performance.

C. As a teacher using this technique or strategy, I added some ideas of my own as you might certainly do. I developed a procedure that I used daily in almost every fiction/nonfiction reading I did. I combined the strategies in D.R.T.A.'s (Direct Reading Thinking Activity)and Reciprocal Teaching. This is the procedure I developed:

    1. To introduce the procedure, list the following strategies on the board or chart paper:

        a. Using prior knowledge. (Brainstorming)

        b. Predicting. (Whole book, story, or page by page when warranted by clues)

        c. Questioning. (Teach how to ask open-ended, thought provoking questions)

d. Clarifying. (Give examples of why you need to be sure on each page of a story, what the story is about, what the words mean, and so forth)

e. Summarizing. (Teach children what the main points of a story or nonfiction are and how to recognize them and record them in as few sentences as possible, and also explain story sense, sequencing, and story grammar to them at the same time.)

f. Bridging. (What I like to call the "so what" of the story when you discuss the universal message: why the characters did what they did, why this is important to us, how we may have had a similar experience, what we did differently, and our reflections in general about the story.)

2. Model each of these strategies in a role-playing manner by introducing them one at a time.

a. Prior knowledge

   (1) Hold up the book you're going to use (be sure your students are sitting in front of you or as close to you as possible to avoid distractions).

   (2) Ask what they know about the story or subject matter. (It's important to have chart paper to list these ideas and record them as you sit in front of the youngsters.)

   (3) After compiling your list, suggest you read together now to find out if the ideas they mentioned are in the book.

   (4) After reading a page or two, you might stop and identify the ideas that you read about that are listed on the chart paper and underline them. Then you might also see if anyone noticed something that was not listed and have them list it on the chart.

b. Predicting

   (1) As you read along in text, you might want to only make predictions when the story dictates, such as an abrupt change in plot or a twist or turn that was unexpected. However, this depends on the sophistication or level of your students. Some children need to be kept in tune or alert to even minor happenings or they lose the thread of the story or piece.

   (2) You might want to record some plot predictions as they get more specific. However, many may just echo the prior knowledge items.

   (3) It's important to teach the children about predicting from the organization of the text so that the students begin to look at how the writer sets up titles and subtitles, chapters, units, and so on. Or, in the case of fic-

tion, how the writer's style helps you predict his character(s) actions. Many children never use this valuable tool.

c. Questioning

(1) While you're reading, you will need to frequently ask questions and as you do, point out how the way in which you ask a question determines how much you learn. You need to teach open-ended questioning by modeling it.

(2) Question on every page or even paragraph with young children to keep them interested and listening.

d. Clarifying is the next area to teach by modeling.

(1) It's important when teaching clarifying that you assume the role of the student and read the page looking for vocabulary that may be difficult or sentence structure that is confusing.

(2) When you find either difficult words or confusing parts, you should ask if anyone can explain them. (Children give better explanations to their peers than adults do.) Next you need to read together the words or parts in context to make sure everyone understands, also giving your explanation.

e. Summarizing is the next strategy to model.

(1) A good way to begin teaching children about summarizing is to list important things you've learned after each page. You can prioritize the important information by saying, "Which is more important to this story—this or this?"

(2) How many pages elapse before you stop and list information depends on the text and how many really important issues there are.

(3) When you are finished reading you will then look over your list of important issues and prioritize again.

(4) The last skill you want your students to learn is to be as succinct as possible. So you might want to go back over the sentences and combine or condense them. Because of the importance of this skill, you will want the children to start doing this, on their own, as soon as possible. You can start doing it as a large group with your guidance. Then have a small group with a child as a teacher (that you know is competent). Practice doing this for a period of time until everyone can show they can do it.

f. Bridging, or the "so what" of reading, is the last area to model. This area, too, is a very important one. It causes students to reflect on what they've read and ponder the connections to other things they've read or, better yet, to their own experiences and lives. It's always important to connect as much book learning to real life situations as possible. Many youngsters don't do this unless they're taught to do it. Ask the following:

(1) What do you think the author was telling us in this story?

(2) Have you ever had anything like this happen to you? Did it end the same way?

(3) Have you ever read about a similar situation or seen something on TV like this?

(4) What do you think is the most important lesson or information in this story?

(5) How can we write about or reflect on this? (Make a list of ways on board or chart paper.)

II. What is meant by a system for learning in reading and writing?

Remember when implementing these strategies that you develop one consistent system at the beginning of the year. Model it every day as clearly as you can. As soon as the students are comfortable with the system, allow them to do it themselves without your input. But, a word to the wise ... you may have to continue modeling longer with some of your students. It's extremely crucial that all your students understand this system before you have them try it on their own. They will not work on their own unless they're sure of what to do. It's worth the extra time it takes to be sure they understand. You may want to enlist the aid of those who are sure of the system to assist you in helping those who are not. But, again, be careful who you choose to assist you. It can be damaging to self-esteem if the student you choose is at all patronizing to those they assist. And also be sure to model the system when doing any whole class lesson.

The steps to follow are:

A. Direct teaching of one particular system or strategy that you've devised or one that fits your teaching/learning style.

1. Using Prior Knowledge: 2. Predicting:	> Before Reading
3. Questioning: 4. Clarifying:	> During Reading
5. Summarizing: 6. Bridging (So What?):	> After Reading

TABLE 3–1
Reading
Strategies

FIGURE 3–1 Before Reading Strategies Map

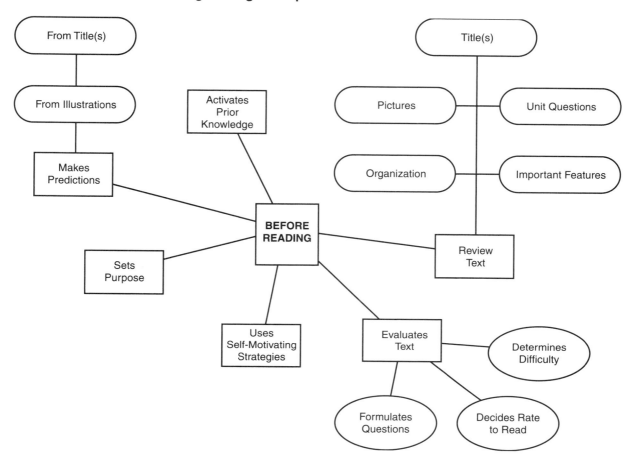

B. Be consistent; use the system every time you do a reading lesson of any kind whether it's science, social studies, language arts, and so forth.

C. Have the children practice using the system first with your input and assistance and then on their own in groups with you just helping when they request it.

D. Do not expect all students will learn the system and become independent at the same time. (It's better to err on the side of too much practice than not enough.)

E. Do encourage the development of other systems or strategies, of their own—derived from yours—that suits their metacognitive style. Students probably will not even consider this until the latter part of the year, and even then it will probably be only a handful of your better or more independent youngsters. Be sure when they suggest doing this that you ask them to model it for you and caution them to be consistent in its use.

FIGURE 3–2   During Reading Strategies Map

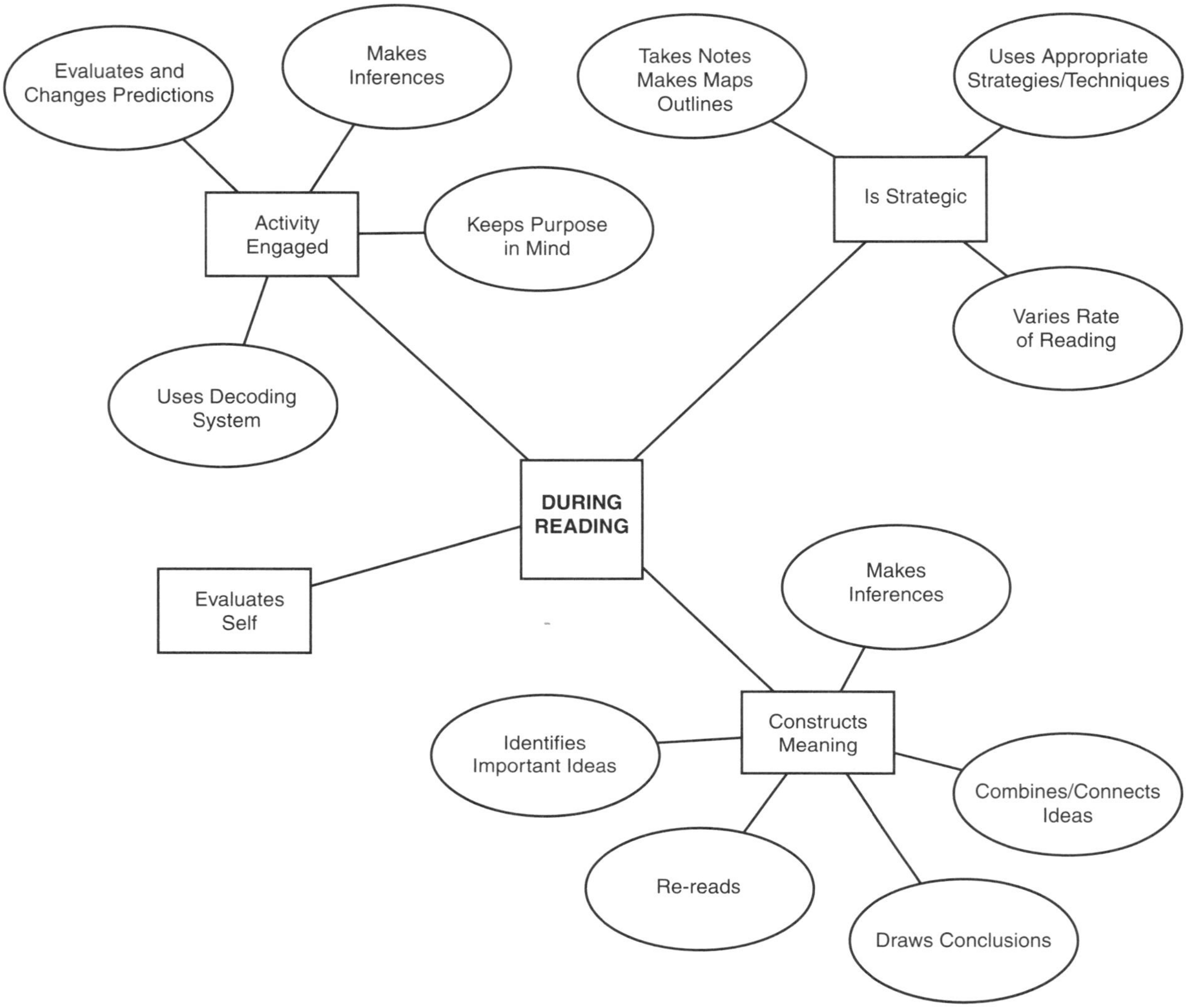

III. What are the researched, tried and true strategies that really work in developing better readers and writers?

There are other strategies to use for various kinds of reading lessons you provide for your students. These will contribute to their ability to be self-directed and able to learn on their own and will also encourage the reading/writing connection that is important in literacy. As we begin to discuss the strategies you need to use with your children, keep in mind that you also need to develop extended lessons that will be appropriate for all levels of ability. You always need to include writing and to model the writing process over and over again at the beginning of the year. Let us begin by reviewing the writing process. I would suggest that you model all stages of the

FIGURE 3–3   After Reading Strategies Map

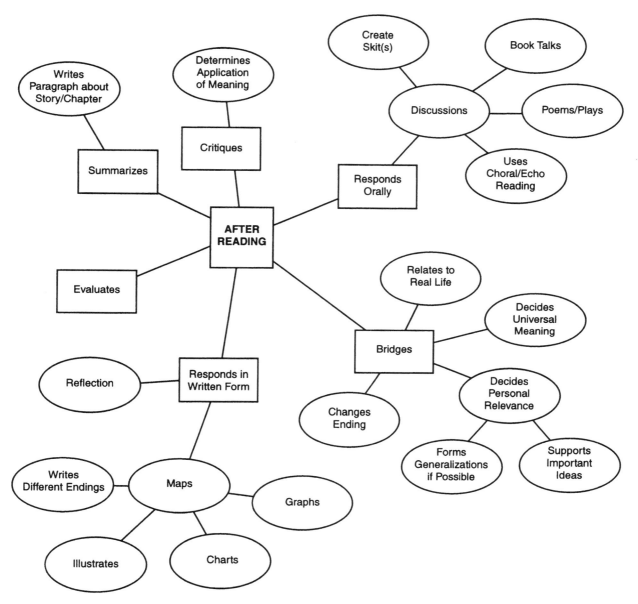

process at the beginning of the year. You need to do it as a group until the students are familiar with each step. Then do some practice in small groups as you did with the reading system you developed.

Modeling—Begin by:

A. Brainstorming or use of prior knowledge.

   1. Children need to spend a lot of time talking before they ever put pen to paper. Having a scheduled time for discussion every

day about a wide range of topics is the way to begin the year. Gradually get more specific about a theme you're developing or a single topic you want to study. The important issue is to not be premature about beginning writing. Doing a web together or letting children work in a small group on a single topic is a good starting place. Remember to provide many books, magazines, and reference books, as it is crucial to pique their curiosity with interesting facts and ideas. Just having a general show-and-tell session of what's happening in their lives and jotting down thoughts on the board or in journals is a good beginning. Again, the important thing is consistency, and having children practice and observe you modeling is the key to learning.

2. Another idea for fiction is using writing prompts when you start the process. You can either write sentences on the board such as, "It was a dark, cold, and windy night as he walked along the pathway by the turbulent sea. Suddenly, the sound of a bloodcurdling scream reached his ears. What was that? Was it a person? Did it come from behind him? Where could he run? And then he heard a sound right in back of him." Then have the children finish the story by themselves or in small groups and discuss them when completed. Do this often as the children get ready to begin writing on their own.

B. Drafting—the first attempt at writing on their own.

Once you are sure your children are ready to write, the drafting should begin. Provide the youngsters with lots of different kinds of writing materials and review all the things you've done together. Encourage them by going around the room and making suggestions, if asked, or reminding them of something they shared during discussion time, or something they told you, or an interest you know they have in sports or animals, and so on.

Many times, even after weeks of modeling and practice writing drafts together, you'll still have some reluctant writers. They may ask to work with a partner. Be sure this is temporary or they will never risk doing it on their own. I often sit with the children myself and continue to help them get started offering to write some sentences with them. Praising their attempts is so important to getting them to risk trying!

C. Revising—going over your work to make it better.

Establishing a trusting, nonjudgmental atmosphere for revising is crucial. You will never be successful in process writing if you allow children to criticize each other's writing without being constructive. You need to be sure when you're modeling revising that you talk about revisions and write a story for the students to revise so they understand and practice revising as a process to improve.

Discuss the following points using real pieces of literature:

• Why do we need punctuation?

• How can we say something clearly? What words do we use to explain or clarify a point?

• How do we organize ideas, and so forth?

- What is a topic sentence? Why is the first sentence in your piece so important? How do we use it in nonfiction as well as fiction?

- How important is it to start the story with a sentence that grabs your interest?

After you've followed these preliminary steps, it's important now to have them "plunge in" on their own. By this time, if you've modeled enough and established a safe, trusting environment, you should have very few students unable to proceed. However, there are always a few that are timid and insecure and just need a little individual encouragement. So, as they start writing, look for those students (you probably already know who they are). Go over and sit with them, ask questions, read over their drafts with them, have them work again with partners, if necessary. It all depends on the particular class you have. Remember, at some point though, they must practice this skill on their own, if you really want to have independent writers.

On Their Own

D. Drafting

Drafting is the development, organization, and recording of ideas and thoughts you've discussed orally or to yourself. Students need to use inventive spelling, drawing, or any other means with which they're comfortable to express their ideas. They could use tape recorders or dictate to aides if they're too young to do it on their own or are not comfortable doing so. However, let me sound a bit of caution here. You need to encourage students to communicate their ideas in whatever form they find is best and not push them too quickly into writing in the conventional sense. The stages of writing are necessary and some children move more slowly through them than others. Students need to do the following:

1. Think of a topic.

2. Use inventive spelling, if necessary.

3. Make a web or record ideas, feelings, experiences.

4. Create images, connect thoughts.

5. Share writing with others.

6. Read and research.

B. Revising

Revising is seeing your writing through another person's eyes. It entails reorganization as well as stylistic changes. Only important and selected pieces should be subjected to revision. Children themselves need to make that determination. It differs from proofreading in that it is not limited to just grammatical changes, punctuation, capitalization, and so forth. Students need to:

1. Share writing with others.

2. Add or change ideas.

3. Restructure sentences and paragraphs.

4. Reconsider language using dictionaries or thesauruses (if children are able to do this).

C. Proofreading

Proofreading is the point at which children need to make their piece grammatically correct. Spelling, punctuation, usage, and so on are all addressed. Students need to:

1. Correct spelling using a dictionary or other people to point out misspelled words (word processors or computers, of course, are the best way to proofread).

2. Correct punctuation and capitalization.

3. Check handwriting for legibility (if not using a computer or word processor).

4. Correct indentations, margins, and so forth.

5. Look for run-on sentences or other mistakes not caught during the revising stage.

Remember to let children work together if they want to, but be very cognizant of helping them become independent and, again, encourage them to do this alone. In our world today, children need to be able to work together and alone so it's important to give them practice in cooperative learning, but also encourage independence as well. How that is accomplished in your classroom depends on the individuals that are in it. You must make those decisions based on your knowledge of the students. Just be sure to give practice in both.

D. Publishing

Publishing is the final step. Only the most important pieces children write will ever reach this stage. Although it is important for children to carry some pieces through to completion, limited time, effort, and value need to be considered. Most youngsters need the practice of doing as much brainstorming, drafting, and shared revising as possible rather than publishing everything they compose. Often creating a class book satisfies this need to see their piece completed and takes less time as the teacher can do the publishing. Students will:

1. Add illustrations.

2. Create a cover.

3. Share writing with classmates or school through writer's fair or some schoolwide affair that promotes publishing children's work.

4. Display writing in the classroom or school building.

5. Read each other's books at scheduled, self-selected reading times.

(See end of chapter for "Establishing a Publishing Center.")

EXTENDING LESSONS PART I

Whenever you start a lesson of any kind in your room, you must be cognizant of the many levels of ability. If you have too many lessons that are too difficult for your students, you will set up an atmosphere of failure. It is much better to err on the side of too much explanation or discussion than too little. Let's pretend you're going to use *The True Story of the Three Little Pigs* by J. Scieszka to read and model a D.R.T.A. lesson for comprehension. Here are some suggestions to extend the lesson for all your students to participate:

1. Have your students sit in front of you at your gathering place.

2. Hold up the book and ask students to tell you what they think the book may be about. Write ideas on the board or on chart paper.

3. Discuss briefly the title page, author, illustrator, dedication, or any other thing you consider important for them to learn.

4. Begin reading in an exaggerated manner with as much expression and enthusiasm as you can (practice reading before hand to know the story and be prepared for important times in the plot.) This ensures your students will listen. If a child becomes inattentive, stop and do not read on until he or she is listening once more. Don't say anything when you stop—just look at the child.

5. Do not stop for questions as often as you do for guided reading, but enough for them to comment and to be sure they're following the plot of the story.

6. When you are finished, discuss your predictions, if you have not done so, and have a general discussion about the story. Don't make this too structured unless they are not commenting on their own. Then you might ask such things as, "Why do you think the author wrote this book from the standpoint of the wolf? If you were the author, how would you write it differently? How is this book like the other story of the three little pigs? How is it different?" (You might want to refresh their memory by reading parts of that story or reminding them of parts of the story. You could also read it in its entirety the day before.)

7. Next, ask the children how they could share this story with other people. Enlist as many ways as possible and list them on the board or on chart paper. When you have exhausted their ideas, you can add any you think are important.

8. Then you need to have the children pick the way they're most comfortable sharing and group according to idea. If you have some students who prefer to work on their own, by all means let them because you want to foster independence as soon as possible in the school year. And, having children model this is important.
    Here are some ideas generated by children for this story.

1. Compare/contrast this story with the original *Three Little Pigs*.

2. Tell familiar story *(Red Riding Hood, Cinderella, etc.)* from another point of view: take a character and tell it through his eyes. Tell about an incident in your life where there is more than one point of view.

3. Discuss favorite "foods."

4. Discuss birthdays. What did you do on your birthday? Did someone have a cake for you?

5. What does it mean to borrow or lend, etc.? Have you ever borrowed anything? Have you ever lent anything?

6. Discuss houses. Why did the straw-stick house collapse (Science)? Why do we use particular building materials? Are they different in different areas of the country? Why? Name some different kinds of houses. Build houses of stick and straw. Make clay models.

7. What happened to "Granny" in the story? What it a lie that he was baking a cake for her? Why do people lie? Which story do you believe? Why would the wolf lie or the pig lie?

8. Placing blame: Were you ever blamed for something you did not do?

9. Court trial: Divide group into pigs/wolves. Who is telling the truth? Why do you believe that person? Debate: Write a true story of the event.

10. Do reporters always tell the "true" story? Do you believe everything you read in the magazines and newspapers? On TV?

11. Identify mathematical concepts in the story. Formulas, imaginary number values, math relationships. Divide in groups to further explore concepts and write. Three (groups chosen) in each group.

12. Change the endings in this story and some other familiar stories.

13. Discuss characters mentioned but not developed. What would they say about the events?

14. Make up a play/skit: "A Trial of the Big Bad Wolf" with judge, witnesses, lawyers, jury. Draw pictures of trial. Role-play pig/wolf.

15. What did the wolf do in jail? Did he have to stay in a long time? Did he ever get out?

16. Making excuses when bad things happen—relate to students' life.

17. Write a letter to A.T. Wolf. Tell him why you agree or do not agree with his version of the story.

18. Discuss a time you got into trouble. Make up a story to explain what *really* happened.

19. What is "persuasive writing"? Discuss what is meant by an "opinion."

20. Discuss real-life stories students see or hear on TV or radio, news events, or how they feel about a situation that happened to them.

21. Do story grammar: sequential events, characters, actions, outcomes.

22. Vary for different levels. Discuss credibility. What should punishment be?

23. Talk about how stories change from repetition—play operator—discuss exaggeration.

24. What was funny about this story? What would it feel like to be a pig when the wolf came to the door?

TABLE 3–2
Ideas Generated From
The True Story of the
Three Little Pigs

EXTENDING LESSONS PART II

Using *Alfie Gets In First* by S. Hughes Morrow, 1981.

A. Procedure Day One

1. Make a list of words from the story that tell some facts from the beginning, middle, and end.

2. Write story grammar headings on board or on chart paper.

3. Have children insert vocabulary words where they think they should go.

4. Tell the story from the headings and title.

5. Read the story commenting on the predictions as you read along. Make new predictions as well.

6. Discuss things that have happened to them that are like the events in the story.

B. Procedure Day Two

1. Review important story elements; compare to other stories read.

2. Reflect on story and write summary.

IV. How can I help create a feeling in my students that they are readers and writers?

I have listed below the ways I've used in my own classroom to create these feelings:

A. Create comfort by being nonjudgmental and by encouraging children to express their true thoughts and feelings.

B. Explain and model. Give directions clearly and repeat until you're sure children understand. Model strategies every day. Then let children experiment with making their own strategies that fit their particular and unique learning styles.

C. Allow time for direct teaching and lots of practice, practice, practice.

D. Praise effort. Be sure it's worth praising or children will think you don't know them very well. (Your standards for praise need to match their ability to do the task, not some standard that is beyond their capabilities.)

E. Be enthusiastic in everything you do. Remember, if you don't care, neither will they.

F. Listen, don't talk. Limit the amount of talking you do. Teach by example. Talk only when teaching a new concept or idea that needs oral explanation.

G. Answer a question with a question. When children ask you a question, instead of giving them a quick answer, say, "What do you think?"

H. Work along with them. Sit next to individuals or a group of children coaching and encouraging them.

I. Give immediate feedback. Train parent volunteers or older students to assist you in giving feedback to students. Walk around the room as children work and evaluate what they're doing by making suggestions. Teach other classmates to be checkers in a positive, noncritical way. Don't carry papers home to grade. You're missing the crucial ingredient—the discussion with the children about why they answered as they did.

J. Be observant and consistent. Set up a system for observing your children on a daily basis. Notice how they approach tasks and learn their personal learning habits, interests, and feelings so that you can help them become independent learners. Be consistent in everything you do at the beginning of the year so children know what to expect.

K. Thinking out loud (reading). One of the important ways to help students become independent is to let them see how you think. When students are provided with a glimpse of your reasoning and thinking, it helps them develop their own reasoning and thinking skills (Davey, 1983).[3]

Here is how I used this strategy while teaching either a reading or writing lesson.

1. Let's pretend I'm reading a story just for fun, but I want the children to see how I think about it as I read. The book I've chosen is *The Whingdingdilly* by Bill Peet (a favorite of mine).

   a. I would begin this book just as I do a guided reading lesson by holding up the book and making a prediction. However, I would be the one making the prediction and telling why I thought as I did. For example:

      (1) "I see a really funny looking animal—it must be the Whingdingdilly! I wonder how it got like that? Looks like it has zebras' and elephants' legs, a hump like that on a camel, antlers like a deer's, ears like an elephant and a nose like a rhinoceros. Boy! Is he ever funny looking! And he looks so sad. Maybe this book will be about how he got to look that way and why he's so sad. I think he'll be okay in the end because children's stories usually have a happy ending. But I know there will be a lot of problem solving and adventures first."

      (2) "Let's begin reading starting with the title page. I like to see who wrote the book because if I like it, I might want to read another one of the author's books. I see a boy, a beautiful white horse, and a sad looking dog. He looks as sad as the Whingdingdilly on the cover. The boy sure seems interested in the horse. The horse looks

like he's strutting—very proud of himself. This book is written and illustrated by Bill Peet, which means he wrote it and also drew the pictures. I wonder how many authors write and illustrate their books?"

(3) Page 1—"Boy, there's that sad little dog again laying on a porch. I hope this page tells why he's so sad." (Read page.) "I guess mournful must mean like mourning or grieving—I've heard the word 'mourned' before. No one knows, I guess, why this old farm dog, Scamp, is so miserable. It seems like it hasn't always been the case. I guess he used to be happy. Maybe something happened to him. I hope we find out."

(4) Pages 2 and 3—"Now we know why he's so sad. He's really jealous of the horse. I know that it's sometimes hard not to be jealous about something. Especially since the white horse is so much bigger and I'm sure he thinks much more beautiful. I bet this story is going to be about how Scamp gets over his jealousy and is happy again with who he is."

(5) Pages 4 and 5—"No wonder Scamp is jealous. Everyone seems to really admire that white horse, Palomar. And no one pays attention to him. When people or animals feel unloved, they're sad."

(6) Pages 6 and 7—"Oh, poor Scamp. He thought if he could act like Palomar and strut around, everyone would notice and admire him. Now, his best friend in the world, Orvie, is laughing at him. It hurts to be laughed at, so now he's going to run away. I sure wish he'd just be himself and not try to be someone else. It really never works. I guess I'm reminded of the saying 'the grass is always greener on the other side of the fence.' But it really isn't."

b. You need to proceed through the book like this, taking whatever time is necessary. Remember, you're modeling a strategy and helping children see exactly how you do it. You don't need to do it very often. But, when you do, be sure you take the time to do it well.

L. Thinking out loud (writing)

1. In order to inspire children to write you must first read, read, read and experience first-hand the sights, smells, tastes, and feel of what you're going to write about. For example, rather than say, "It's a wonderful spring day. I'm going to write about the first day of spring," instead take them outside for a walk where you point out how the air feels and what you see using words such as crisp, cool, new-mown grass smells, colored bugs, worms wiggling, birds pecking, ants crawling, and so on. Read them many stories and poems picked for descriptive and exciting language, and be sure to call attention to those words,

phrases, and so forth. Bring in an object, such as a bird nest, an empty cocoon, or a snake's skin. Let the children feel them and then you speculate on what might have been in them. Show the children how you put ideas together and write a poem or story for them on chart paper or on the board showing carefully how you choose beginning sentences and words that are appropriate. Talk them through everything you write.

2. Before you ever ask children to write themselves, you must be sure you model how you write so that they can see and learn techniques that will help them.

> Remember: the more you read, the better you write and the better you write, the more you want to read.

M. Graffiti murals or boards

Have your children create a mural around your room. You can make it an events mural for everything you do (for example, themes, social studies, science, reading responses). Or it can be a timeline indicating the projects/activities you've done starting with September/October and going around your room ending with May or June. It's a great way to celebrate learning and show children how much they've accomplished. You can also create a wall in your room for the following things.

1. Brainteasers: such as "explain chocolate, mustard, pancake syrup" to someone who has never tasted those things.

2. A word a day: to define without a dictionary, such as tremulous, pirouette, frangipani (words that children might find interesting and challenging). Of course, it will depend on your grade level as to how difficult the words would be but all children should be exposed to a word a day for the challenge and fun it creates.

3. Poems that excite the mind: look for funny ones like those found in Shel Silverstein's book *Where the Sidewalk Ends*, or M. A. Hoberman's *A House is a House for Me*, or *A Sky Full of Poems* by E. Merriam for various kinds of poems.

4. New words: have children put up words they've learned that were particularly difficult or hard to learn. (You will need to monitor this board and set some rules about the kind of words chosen or it could get out of hand.)

5. Words for story making: put six or eight words you'd like your children to learn and have them make up stories with them. (Use partners for this as the stories will be more interesting if you do.)

6. Unusual words to pronounce: assign pairs of children to try to sound the words out. Save it until the end of the day when

they then reveal the pronunciation. This is good for children to practice syllabication. Make them extra-long words that have many syllables. (You can also assign children this job each week letting one or a pair of students find the words.)

7. Interesting people: list names of people in the news from the political, entertainment, or academic world. Then provide encyclopedias, magazines, and newspapers to find out who they are, what they've done, and so forth. I always included interviewing people such as the principal, other teachers, custodians, secretaries, and other school staff, for this information (with their prior consent, of course).

8. Interesting phrases, sayings, puns, idioms, jokes, and so forth.

9. Nonsense words for students to give meaning to by defining them.

V. What role does phonics play in developing readers and writers?

Teaching children the letter/sound relationship in our language is important. The area of disagreement among the experts in the reading/writing field has more to do, generally, with how to teach it. Following are some ways to develop decoding ability in your students. You will need to adjust the level to fit your age students.

A. Steps to developing decoding knowledge

Test the ability of your children by having them write a paragraph for you as you dictate it. Have the words contain all the consonant sounds in our language {B C D F G (hard and soft) H J K L M N P Q U R S T V W X Y Z} .

1. The paragraph may look like this (about third grade level): Be sure to listen when people talk to you. Follow the rules in the classroom. Do your homework the day it's given to you. Question freely. Just be yourself and value others. Give extra attention to detail. Have a zest for living and be generous and sincere. (Remember to look only at the beginning letters of these words and not the total spelling, although that will provide other clues you may want to consider.)

2. If your children know the sounds of the consonants, you can then move on to vowel patterns. If they do not know the sounds, provide practice. Do not do the sounds in isolation but rather include them in words to learn such as rhyming words, words for a personal word bank, or read books such as controlled vocabulary readers that include simple words to practice the sounds. Be sure to do direct teaching for this practice.

3. Teach or review vowel patterns by creating words containing vowel patterns. Do not attempt to teach vowels (A E I O U and sometimes Y) in isolation. Having a board containing words in your room provides word practice on a daily basis and not only helps students learn vowels, but also helps in the practice of consonant sounds. Following are the beginning and advanced spelling/vowel patterns used by the Benchmark School in Pennsylvania (1986).[4] The school also sells a bound program suggest

ing ways to teach these spelling/vowel patterns and how to use a word wall (see the end of the chapter page for the address of the school. They also have some recent research concerning the use of this program). See suggestions for using a word wall below—some are from the Benchmark School and some are my own adaptations.

TABLE 3–3 Spelling Patterns, Beginning (c. Benchmark School, 1986)

Appendix: Spelling-Pronunciation Matches for BWI Key Words

Listed below are the matches between spellings and pronunciations for the key words that are taught in the Benchmark School Beginning Word Identification Program—Revised. The words are listed in the order they are introduced, from Week 1 to Week 28 in phase II of the program. Each word's spelling is written in uppercase letters first and its pronunciation is written in lowercase letters beneath. Spellings and pronunciations are segmented into letter units and sound units separated by blank spaces with vertical lines to indicate matches. The number of letter-sound matches within each word is written after the pronunciation (bottom line). In addition to lowercase letters, a few special symbols are used to designate sounds. Long vowels saying their own letter names are topped by a horizontal bar; short vowels are unmarked. Other vowels are indicated by two letters underlined to represent one sound. Schwa vowels are represented by the letter U. The purpose of the pronunciation symbols is to clarify how we segment words into sounds and the identities of the sounds. These symbols are not taught to students. Readers should note that this analysis assumes a dialect that may not characterize all readers.

In the course of encountering key words and analyzing constituent letter units and sound units to achieve an optimal match, some complexities arise. These are addressed by structuring lessons and reading materials in such a way that student word detectives will discover the following:

1. Some letters combine to match up to a single sound, among them the following doubled consonants and vowels: NG, CK, CH, TH, SH, PH, WH, WR, KN, OA, OU, OW, OI, OY, AW, AI, AY, EA, EW, IE, IGH, AGH, AUGH, TI, CI, GU.

2. A few words have silent letters that do not match any sound within a specific word, although they may match sounds in other words: L in TALK, L in COULD, final silent E; these letters are marked with an asterisk below.

3. Final E is very often a silent letter that occurs when the preceding vowel says its own name.

4. Vowel letters preceding R match up to a separate vowel sound that is barely heard, for example, E in HER.

5. In some words such as LITTLE, the final letters L and E match up to sounds /u/ and /l/ but the letters reverse the order of the sounds.

6. X may match up to two sounds /ks/, as in TAX.

Complexities (4) and (5) above are taught in this way to conform to the general principle that every chunk or syllable in a word has to have both a vowel sound and a vowel spelling.

```
wk 1     I N              A N D            U P
         | |              | | |            | |
         I N 2            a n d 3          u p 2

wk 2     K I NG           L O NG           J U M P
         | |  |           | |  |           | | | |
         k i  ng 3        l o  ng 3        j u m p 4

wk 3     L E T            P I G            D AY
         | | |            | | |            | |
         l e t 3          p i g 3          d ā 2
```

(Cont.)

TABLE 3–3 *(Cont.)*

Partner-Sharing Chart

Making Words

Person #1:

1. My word is _____ .

2. My new word is _____ .

3. I made this word because I know
_____ .

4. Do you agree?

Person #2:
Give one of these answers:
Yes/No, because _____ .

Switch roles.

*If you finish early, pick other word-wall words
and make them into new words.*

Wk 4	T R U CK — t r u k 4	B L A C K — b l a k 4	N O T — n o t 3	
Wk 5	C A T — k a t 3	I T — i t 2	G O — g ō 2	L OO K — l oo k 3
Wk 6	R E D — r e d 3	F U N — f u n 3	H E — h ē 2	
Wk 7	N A M E* — n ā m e 3	S W I M — s w i m 4	M Y — m ī 2	M A P — m a p 3
Wk 8	C A R — k au r 3	V I N E* — v ī n 3	S EE — s ē 2	C A N — k a n 3
Wk 9	T E N T — t e n t 4	R OU N D — r ou n d 4	S K A T E* — s k ā t 4	T E N — t e n 3
Wk 10	O L D — ō l d 3	F R O G — f r o g 4	R IGH T — r ī t 3	
Wk 11	S L I D E* — s l ī d 4	S T O P — s t o p 4	T E LL — t e l 3	H E R — h u r 3
Wk 12	A N — a n 2	S M A SH — s m a sh 4	B R A V E* — b r ā v 4	
Wk 13	C OW — k ou 2	S L EE P — s l ē p 4	S C OU T — s k ou t 4	

(Cont.)

TABLE 3–3   *(Cont.)*

Wk 14	F O R	A LL	S AW	
	f o r 3	au l 2	s au 2	

Wk 15	H A D	K I CK	S N AI L	G L O W
	h a d 3	k i k 3	s n ā l 4	g l ō 3

Wk 16	B OA T	TH I N K	N E S T	
	b ō t	th i ng k 4	n e s t 4	

Wk 17	T R EA T	M A K E*	TH A N K	
	t r ē t 4	m ā k 3	th a ng k 4	

Wk 18	M I C E*	L I TT L E	M O R E*	
	mi s 3	l i t u l 5	m o r 3	

Wk 19	SH I P	C L O CK	W A SH	S T A TI O N
	sh i p 3	k l o k 4	w au sh 3	s t ā sh u n 6

Wk 20	S K U N K	WH A L E*	B OY	B A B Y
	s k u ng k 5	w ā l 3	b oi 2	b ā b ē 4

Wk 21	S Q U I R T	S CH OO L	C OU L* D	
	s k w u r t 6	s k oo l	k oo d 3	

Wk 22	C AUGH T	C OI N	T A L* K	
	k au t 3	k oi n 3	t au k 3	

Wk 23	P A G E*	F L EW	F L U	
	p ā j 3	f l oo 3	f l oo 3	

Wk 24	U S E*	B U G	R AI N	
	ū s 2	b u g	r ā n 3	
	ū z 2			

Wk 25	P A L	F U R	P L A C E*	
	p a l 3	f u r 3	p l ā s 4	

Wk 26	PH O N E*	Q U EE N	W R I T E*	
	f ō n 3	k w ē n 4	r ī t 3	

(Cont.)

TABLE 3–3   *(Cont.)*

Wk 27

KNIFE* → n ī f   3
PLANE* → p l ā n   4
GU E SS → g e s   3

Wk 28

BABIES → b ā b ē z   5
TAX → t a k^s   4
DELICIOUS → d ē l i sh u s   7

Spelling Patterns, Advanced (c. Benchmark School, 1986)

	- a		- e		- i		- o		- u
	A	h	e	(an)	i(mals)	(choc)	o(late)	fl	u
gr	ab	s	ea	h	i	g	o	cl	ub
t	able	b	each	(mat)er	ial	c	oach	b	uck
M	ac	h	ead	(spec)	ial	r	oad	tr	uck
pl	ace	sp	eak	r	ib	g	oak	m	ud
bl	ack	r	eal	tr	ibe	f	oal	n	ude
f	act	scr	eam	(pos)s	ible	m	oam	j	udge
h	ad	cl	ean	t	ic	r	oan	gl	ue
m	ade	ch	eap	m	ice	c	oar	p	uff
st	aff	l	earn	k	ick	b	oast	b	ug
r	aft	y	ear	d	id	j	oat	m	ule
fl	ag	tr	eat	sl	ide	r	ob	r	ule
p	age	w	eb	p	ie	d	obe	p	ull
p	aid	r	ec	ch	ief	r	oc	g	ull
sn	ail	s	ect	(ba)b	ies	cl	ock	dr	um
	air	r	ed	kn	ife	n	od	j	ump
r	ain	(centi)p	ede		if	r	ode	f	un
r	aise	s	ee	cl	iff		off	l	unch
b	ait	bl	eed	g	ift	fr	og	J	une
m	ake	w	eek	(iden)t	ify	(ecol)	ogy	h	ung
di	al	f	eel	p	ig		oil	sk	unk
p	al	s	eem	r	ight		oin	h	unt
wh	ale	qu	een	l	ike	c	oke		up
t	alk	sl	eep	sm	ile	br	old	f	ur
	all	b	eer	w	ill		ole	s	ure
	am	sw	eet	t	ilt	h	oll	b	um
n	ame	l	eft	sw	im	d	oll	n	urse
ch	amp	l	eg	t	ime	r	olt		us
c	an	w	eigh		in	c	olve	r	use
d	ance	g	eight	s	ince	s	om	j	ush
	and	(jew)	el	f	ind	T	om	b	ust
pl	ane	t	el	(medi)c	ine	fr	ome	fl	ut
b	ang	b	ell	(subma)	rine	h	ome	b	ute
ch	ange	th	elt	v	ine	c	on		uzz
th	ank	t	em	k	ing	drag	on		
pl	ant	f	en	th	ink	ph	one		
m	ap		ence	pr	int	l	ong		
sh	ape		end	(sta)t	ion	z	oo		
gr	aph	sc	ene	(cur)	ious	g	ood		
c	ar	t	ent	sh	ip	f	ood		
w	ar	st	ep	p	ipe	l	ook		
h	ard	h	er	s	ir	sch	ool		
c	are	v	er(y)	f	ire	r	oom		
sh	ark	s	erve	g	irl	s	oon		
f	arm	th	ese	squ	irt	tr	oop		
b	arn	y	es	h	is	f	oot		

-	y
m	y
(ba)b	y
t	ype

(Cont.)

48 **Chapter 3**

TABLE 3–3 *(Cont.)*

-	*a*	-	*e*	-	*i*	-	*o*	-	*u*
h	arp	dr	ess	th	is	t	oot		
sm	art	n	est	w	ise	st	op		
sc	ary	l	et	w	ish	h	ope		
h	as	P	ete	r	isk	f	or		
b	ase	B	eth	(favorit)	ism	p	orch		
sm	ash	r	ev	m	iss	m	ore		
	ask	fl	ew	l	ist	f	ork		
cl	ass	k	ey		it	f	orm		
f	ast	T	ex	p	itch	c	orn		
c	at			wr	ite	sh	ort		
c	atch			f	ive	n	ose		
sk	ate			g	ive	cr	oss		
b	ath			s	ix	l	ost		
c	aught			wh	iz	m	ost		
sl	av			pr	ize	n	ot		
	av(erage)					n	otch		
br	ave					n	ote		
s	aw					f	ought		
dr	awn					t	ough		
t	ax					c	ould		
d	ay						ounce		
bl	aze					r	ound		
j	azz					c	ount		
						y	our		
						(fa)m	ous		
						h	ouse		
						sc	out		
						s	outh		
						dr	ove		
						l	ove		
						c	ow		
						gl	ow		
						h	owl		
						d	own		
							own		
						b	oy		
						b	ox		

B. Suggestions for making a word wall:

1. Find a bulletin board you can use to put approximately five words a week starting in September/October and continuing through the year. (Some people use the space above the bulletin boards and go across the whole front of the room.)

2. Introduce the five words each week by writing them on colored paper in different shapes.

3. Develop an activity each day with these words such as:

    a. Writing sentences or a story with them.

    b. Making lists of rhyming words or words that have the same vowel pattern. Have children work in pairs and then share their lists with the class.

    c. Have the children practice the words out loud in a choral reading style, saying each letter and clapping. Most words will be one syllable words, but as time goes on, you probably will include harder words with more than one syllable.

    d. Give a spelling test on the words at the end of the week. Make it an informal, self-correcting exercise.

    e. Devise some activities of your own to practice the words through the week. Be sure you spend at least 15 to 20 minutes a day on this word practice no matter what your grade level. For older students, just make the activities harder and the words more difficult.

    f. Use the words on the wall for writing reports or papers of any kind, as the children can use them without having to look up words in a dictionary. They usually learn many more words during the year as well.

4. Be sure you give your children lots of practice reading at their independent reading level. As they read more and more books, they will learn the sound letter association by saying words over and over that contain those sounds.

5. When you read aloud with your children, call attention to sounds letters make. It's especially important to talk about exceptions or multiple sounds letters make.

6. Remember to write every time you read, because as you write in journals or as a response to reading, you can talk with your children about their use of letter sounds and vowel patterns to create words.

7. Have weekly conferences with your children when you not only discuss content and meaning in their work, but also spelling of words. You then can make individual plans to help students learn consonant sounds and vowel patterns they don't know.

8. Enlist the help of older students and parent volunteers to help students learn the sounds they don't know. (It is crucial that you do this no matter how much time it takes.)

VI. What are some activities and ideas for reading and writing in the classroom?

A. School-wide used book fair: children bring in used books from home and trade for another one. Whatever number you bring in, you get back. Steps to follow:

1. Contact parents for help in organization.

2. Limit number of books individual children bring.

3. Set schedule to include early elementary K–3 first and 4–5 or 6 later. Be sure you schedule enough time for classes (two at a time)—30 minutes.

4. Save some books for older students. Don't put out all books at beginning of time.

5. Have collection boxes in every classroom.

6. Sort books into categories for easier viewing: picture books, animal books, authors, and so on.

B. Reading auction: children earn tokens for reading books. Items are collected for the auction while students are reading (5–6 weeks). Then items are auctioned off and children bid on them using their tokens earned for reading.

1. Have children read books that are at their independent level.

2. Decide tokens values by discussing this in class (how many pages, books, and so forth, for tokens).

3. Decide initial value of items to be auctioned.

4. Try to include everyone so that no one leaves without some item no matter how small.

5. Teacher should be auctioneer to keep it organized and fair (at least the first time you have one).

C. Read and share: parents read a certain number of books to their children in a month. The student receives a certificate for each month of participation. Any student participating for 3 months gets a free book from class purchases in a book club such as Trumpett, Scholastic, or others, or from P.T.A. or business groups.

1. Make clear and simple rules about what can be read (include comic books, poems, and other categories).

2. Inform parents of class project. Be clear about purpose. Suggest an older sibling read if parents are really busy, or have students at school in upper grades read to younger students before and after school and at lunch time.

3. Start a book club enrollment early in the year to collect books to give.

4. Don't start this Read and Share until the middle or end of the year when you have collected lots of books. Encourage parents to read to their children, of course, from the beginning of

the year, but it's been my experience that you need many, many books and materials to do this activity.

D. *Ben the Bear* or *Robert the Rabbit*, for example (for grades K–2): Send a stuffed bear, bunny, or other animal, home on weekends with a child. At the end of the weekend, the students and parents write a story of the animal's adventures. The story, along with an illustration, becomes part of an ongoing class book. It is kept in the classroom for self-selected free reading time.

1. Inform parents about what you're doing. Make it clear and simple. Include a sample of how you can write up the adventures. Suggest printing and simple sentences so that students in the class can read it. Be sure you tell them the children will read the adventures independently.

2. Let children and parents pick a weekend together. Don't assign them. (Make schedule and post at beginning of year, preferably on outside of classroom so parents can check dates.)

3. Be sure you let children know that the weekend does not have to include something spectacular, but simply whatever the family enjoys doing together. Benny Bear can enjoy a bedtime story, dinner, TV, a walk around the block, or other activity. You might make a list on the board of things families do together.

E. Take a book: students can take a book home at any time to read and join a book club (see next activity) to share the books read.

1. Each book must be placed in a plastic bag and checked out.

2. Allow children to have at least 15 minutes at the end of each day to do this.

3. Develop a system of putting the names of books on cards and then putting the cards in one box to take them out and one to return them. All they have to do is sign their names (the cards are put in pockets in the books).

4. Inside the cover of each book can be learning activities to try with the book as well.

F. Book club: set up a weekly book club schedule. You can use your free reading time or DEAR (Drop Everything And Read), if you'd like, so that others not involved are busy doing some individual reading.

1. You can either be the moderator or a parent or another student can be in charge.

2. Children read one story together (multiple copies of books you have in the room) or share books they've read for "Take a book."

3. You can have a format of a book talk (just discussing thoughts, plots, or favorite parts) or a guided reading session where children follow these guidelines. If a parent or child is leading the group, prepare them by teaching the following guidelines.

Things to do:

Before reading:

---

1. Ask children to predict what they think is going to happen in the story.

2. Discuss the cover, title, title page, and ask if they recall any other book written by this author.

3. If it's a nonfiction book, ask what things they think they will learn from reading it.

During reading:

---

1. Ask open-ended questions while reading to be sure everyone is understanding the plot.

2. Model expression and fluency by reading one page to them.

3. Clarify the meaning of any vocabulary words you think might be hard for them.

4. Call on students randomly.

5. Comment enthusiastically about the story and interject some comments about what you think may happen. Ask for their opinions. Encourage talking about the events.

After reading:

---

1. Discuss the plot of the story. Compare it to others they might have read.

2. Discuss the author's/universal message.

3. Have general discussion about parts of the story they liked, characters that were interesting, etc.

4. Discuss the idea of writing about the story, drawing a picture to illustrate parts, or any other way of reflecting on the story they may have.

TABLE 3–4
Parent Information
for Book Club

5. Conclude by allowing time to complete this reflection.

6. Fill out Book Club Inventory List individually.

G. Readers for rent: students advertise their reading skills by producing posters. Teachers sign up for the readers for certain hours of the day. Students choose a book and read to the students, or teachers suggest a book ahead of time for students to read.

1. Children must read the book ahead of time and practice expression, fluency, and so forth.

2. You need to devise a form for teachers to sign up and post it in your room. You can do it as follows:

Who?_____ (student's name)

Where?_____ (classroom to read in)

Student Name _____

Date _____

Book Title _____

Author _____

Illustrator _____

Interest comments _____

_____

_____

Group project decision _____

_____

Our project was _____

TABLE 3–5
Book Club
Inventory List
_____

_____

When?_____ (time to read)

What?_____ (the book)

Make schedule to post from these forms.

3. Have students reflect on reading by sharing experiences in class.

H. Storytelling tips:

1. Reading aloud requires preparation and planning. It's important to choose poems or stories about which you are enthusiastic. You can't tell a story well unless you really like it.

2. You need to be able to maintain eye contact as you tell the story. So, it's imperative to really know exactly what you're going to say—practice, practice, practice!

3. The atmosphere in which you tell the story should be informal and pleasant. The children should be seated directly in front of you so they can see and hear you well. Also, if you have pictures to show, this is necessary so everyone can see them clearly.

4. Keep the reading/telling moving smoothly. Allow the children to enjoy the story by pausing for laughter, a few simple questions, comments, but not too many as it will interfere with the story line. Remember these tools of a storyteller:

   - Expressive eyes
   - Facial expressions
   - Pauses
   - Suspense

- Variety in voice, speed, and tone
- A good book
- Lots of rehearsals

I. More strategies for reading

It is well acknowledged that the more responsibility learners assume for their own learning, the more effective the learning experience will be. It's so important to be sure to engage children's active attention. Enjoying the book with them reflecting on the form and content, and varying the genres are ways of doing this. The following idea is one I've used in a classroom: Story structure—Repeated readings aloud of favorite books help students learn elements of narrative text. The five story elements help children visualize how the story progresses, the concepts in the story and the relationship of the elements. The elements are: Setting, Characters, Problem/Goal, Events, and Resolution.

J. Taped-recorded reading

Students need to listen to themselves read. However, you need to set up some guidelines. I had them do recordings three times a year.

1. Have students pick a book that is within their independent range (95–100% word accuracy).

2. Have them rehearse the book or passage with a friend. (Either do a chapter or short book.)

3. Set up a corner of the room for taping during a quiet time (lunch time, after school, during quiet activity in room).

4. Give the tape to the student. Emphasize that this is a way for them to hear themselves and improve their oral reading skills. They are in charge of their own learning.

K. Writer's fair

Children write stories, poems, plays, class books, and so on, during the school year and in May or June present a fair. Each class designs a station in the gym/multipurpose room to display their writing pieces. In some cases, the stations are simply tables set up in a manner that enhances the work.

1. There is a schedule set so that all classes, parents, and staff can visit the displays.

2. The children in each classroom choose representatives to man their stations. This can be revolving so that all students get a chance to be there.

3. It can be a more active presentation of pieces, as well, by setting up times for students to read aloud their special pieces. One year we devised clocks indicating times of performances in the various class display areas.

4. Parents like to volunteer, and we combined a bake sale and popcorn sale one time and had it in the evening.

L. Turn off the TV night and read/write

A night is designated as "Turn Off the TV Night" and everyone who participates brings in a slip of paper indicating they did so along with what they wrote or read. If a class has 75% of it's students participating, they get a popcorn party.

1. Be sure the night is a good choice for most of your parents and not a night when there is a school or neighborhood function. You can also schedule one night a month as well.

2. Local businesses sometimes will sponsor the event and defray some costs.

3. You must have the cooperation of the teachers in the building to make it successful.

4. A list of activities to do as a family that night, or a newsletter that discusses library or civic functions that coincide with that night, is helpful.

5. Children need to share what they did with their classmates. Sometimes this encourages more participation for the next one. And it also encourages more families to seek alternatives to TV on a regular basis. That is the purpose and it needs to be discussed and promoted.

Consistent morning exercises *(15 minutes)**
  (grade appropriate)

Modeling Reading/Writing *(30 minutes)*
  Many different strategies: D.R.T.A.s
  K.W.L.s
  Story Elements
  Etc.

Process Writing/Creative Writing/Journal Writing *(20 minutes)*

Guided Reading *(30 minutes)*
  Multiple copies of trade books
  Basal reading selections

Words Block *(20 minutes)*
  Many different programs for word study/phonics/skills

Self-Selected Reading *(20 minutes)*
  Choice of reading material from books, magazines, informational texts, encyclopedias, etc.

Response to Reading *(30 minutes)*
  Writing
  Poetry
  Drawing
  Drama
  Music
  Choral/Echo Reading
  Special Extended Lessons from Guided Reading

TABLE 3–6
Literacy Morning

* These times are only approximate. The activities can be combined, changed, done three or four times a week, etc. It depends on your class and schedule.

Name _____ *Date* _____

1. What are you interested in? What do you like to do outside school: hobbies, music, sports, for vacation, in the summer? Who are your idols: TV and movie, real life? What kind of humor do you prefer?

2. What are you most successful at doing? Why do you think you're successful at doing that?

3. How do you get yourself interested in an assignment in which the subject is boring to you?

4. What classes are your favorites? Why do you like them?

5. How do you like best to learn? Why do you think this is so?

6. How do you like to receive feedback? (by the teachers, peers, through notes, etc.). Who gives you good feedback now?

7. Do you like to be rewarded for doing well on something? How?

8. If you had to pick your favorite thing to do in school, what would it be?

Teacher comments:

TABLE 3–7
Questions to
Motivate Learning

You can either have a center in your room or help set up one in a room in your building. It is one of the best ways I know to celebrate learning. Students love to see their stories, poems, plays, projects, etc., published.

I have helped teachers to establish a publishing center either in their room or outside of it and it is really a personal decision which one prefers. I have seen both be very successful and rewarding to students.

These steps need to be followed:

I. Publishing center in building:

    A. Meets with teachers to determine needs or preferences about the center.

    B. Put notice in school paper or send home notice advertising for volunteers and supplies.

    C. Check in school for availability of computers or typewriters, binder, laminator, etc.

    D. Set meeting time to train volunteers on procedures, bookmaking, etc. (whatever roles necessary)

    E. Decide on location, hours of operation. (Start with one or two days. Expand if necessary.)

    F. Look over the forms at the end of the chapter (Table 3–9) for more specific procedures.

II. A classroom publishing center:

    A. Determine a place in the room large enough to accommodate supplies, computers, typewriters, or any other equipment necessary.

    B. Write a letter to parents asking for help in assisting students (if your children are too young to do their publishing themselves).

    C. Brainstorm with your students about times to be at the center, how many at one time, rules of behavior, etc.

    D. Do direct teaching in process writing, bookmaking, research techniques, using reference materials, etc. Keep handbooks on grammar, punctuation, and materials for reviewing the direct teaching ideas and strategies you modeled and taught, in the center for easy use. (I would suggest you buy *Writers Express* from Write Source Educational Publishing House or *Write Source 2000,* or *Writers Inc.,* all from Write Source, Box 460, Burlington, Wisconsin 53105.)

    E. Start collecting contact or wallpaper, glue, paste, Scotch tape, scissors, staplers, staples, brads, paper clips, hole puncher, pencils, pens, markers, crayons, paints, shirt cardboards, posterboard, etc. (It helps to ask for some of these supplies in the community either from parents, school, or local businesses.)

    F. Look over forms at the end of the chapter (Table 3–9) for additional suggestions, procedures, etc.

**TABLE 3–8
Establishing a
Publishing Center**

1. Meet with teachers to determine needs or what they want in center.

2. Put notice in paper for: Volunteers and supplies.

3. Check in school for availability of computers, typewriters, binders, laminator, etc.

4. Set up meeting to train volunteers on procedures, bookmaking, etc. (whatever roles necessary).

5. Decide on location, hours of operation.

6. Decide procedures you want to follow. (See Tables 3–9B and 3–9C.)

TABLE 3–9A
Steps to Follow
for Creating a
Publishing Center

Possible supplies: contact or wallpaper, glue, paste, Scotch tape, scissors, staplers, staples, brads, paper clips, hole puncher, pencils, pens, markers, crayons, paints, shirt cardboards, posterboard.

1. Check in office to see how many students have signed up and times they are coming in.

2. Meet with your student and read over child's story, poem, etc.

3. Decide on layout: cover, type of print child would like to have, etc.

4. Help child make covers, type story, poem, or put on computer.

TABLE 3–9B
Publishing Center
Daily Procedures

5. Send story with child or file child's work in storage box if not finished.

Name of teacher: _____

Grade: _____ Room: _____

Instructions to volunteers: _____

_____

_____

How to bind:

    Spiral _____   Rings _____

TABLE 3–9C
Class Book
Instruction

    Staple _____   Brads _____

    Other _____

ENDNOTES

1. Patricia J. Babbs and Alden J. Moe, "Metacognition: A Key for Independent Learning from Text," *The Reading Teacher*. January (1983), pp. 422–426.

2. Annemarie Palincsar and K. Ransom, "From the Mystery Spot to the Thoughtful Spot: The Instruction of Metacognitive Strategies," *The Reading Teacher* 41 (1988), pp. 784–789.

3. B. Davey, "Think-aloud: Modeling the Cognitive Processes of Reading Comprehension," *Journal of Reading,* 27 (1983), pp. 44–47.

4. Irene W. Gaskins and Marjorie Downer, *Benchmark Word Identification / Vocabulary Development Program.* (PA: Benchmark Press, 1986). Benchmark School, 2107 N. Providence Rd., Media, PA 19063.

CHILDREN'S BOOKS

Hoberman, M. A. *A House Is a House for Me*. Viking Penguin, 1978.
Hughes, S. *Alfie Gets in First*. Morrow, 1981.
Merriam, E. *A Sky Full of Poems*. Dell, 1986.
Peet, Bill. *The Whingdingdilly*. Houghton-Mifflin, 1970.
Scieszka, J. *The True Story of the Three Little Pigs*. Viking Penguin, 1989.
Silverstein, Shel. *Where the Sidewalk Ends*. Harper and Row, 1974.

REFERENCES

Babbs, Patricia J., and Moe, Alden J. "Metacognition: A Key for Independent Learning from Text." *The Reading Teacher*. January (1983), pp. 422–426.

Brown, Jean E.; Phillips, Lela B.; Stephens, Elaine C. *Toward Literacy*. Belmont, CA: Wadsworth, 1993.

Clay, Marie M. *The Early Detection of Reading Difficulties*. 3rd ed. Portsmouth, NH: Heinemann, 1985.

Davey, B. "Think-aloud: Modeling the Cognitive Processes of Reading Comprehension." *Journal of Reading,* 27 (1983), pp. 44–47.

Frank, Marjorie. *If You're Trying To Teach Kids to Write You've Gotta Have This Book*. Nashville, TN: Incentive Publications, 1979.

Gaskins, Irene W., and Downer, Marjorie. *Benchmark Word Identification / Vocabulary Development Program*. PA: Benchmark Press, 1986.

Goodman, Kenneth. *Phonics Phacts*. Portsmouth, NH: Heinemann, 1993.

Holdaway, Don. *The Foundations of Literacy*. New York: Ashton Scholastic, 1979.

Hornsby, David; Sukarna, Deborah; Parry, Joann. *Read On: A Conference Approach to Reading*. Portsmouth, NH: Heinemann, 1986.

Hornsby, David; Parry, Joann; and Sukarna, Deborah. *Teach On*. Portsmouth, NH: Heinemann, 1992, pp. 18–23.

Leu, Donald S., Jr., and Kinzer, Charles K. *Effective Reading Instruction K–8*. 2nd ed. New York: Macmillan, 1991.

Routman, Regie. *Invitations: Changing as Teachers and Learners K–12*. Toronto, Canada: Irwin; Portsmouth, NH: Heinemann, 1991.

Tchudi, Susan. *Integrated Language Arts in the Elementary School*. Belmont, CA: Wadsworth, 1994.

Weaver, Constance. *Reading Process and Practice—From Socio-Psycholinguistics To Whole Language*. 2nd ed. Portsmouth, NH: Heinemann, 1994.

CHAPTER 4

Integrating the Curriculum

PHILOSOPHY

Research is leading us in the direction of integrated learning. We recognize, for example, that cooperative learning appears to be more beneficial to learning than is competitive learning (Johnson, Johnson, & Maruyama, 1983).[1] If we understand this, then we can conclude that children working together on assignments and projects is desirable. So, theme development that integrates learning by using the concept of co-operative learning is a good model. But how do we begin to develop themes? What are those important first steps necessary to insure success?

In this chapter understanding themes is the glue that links all the learning. If you do not make your themes broad enough so that your students are really thinking and truly engaged, you will not be successful. So it is very important that your planning is carefully considered.

During my visits to many schools and classrooms, I have seen teachers implementing themes and integrated learning: The questions that are most frequently asked are the ones I will address in this chapter. I will also include some theme webs that I have either seen in classrooms or have developed with my students in my college classes.

LEARNING PRINCIPLES

This chapter will follow the principles of learning listed below:

Principle 2—*Goals of the Learning Process.* The learner seeks to create meaningful and coherent representations of knowledge regardless of the quantity and quality of data available.

Principle 8—*Developmental Constraints and Opportunities.* Individuals proceed through identifiable progressions of physical, intellectual, emotional, and social development that are a function of unique genetic and environmental factors.

We will discuss the following questions:

I.   What is a theme? How do I develop the idea of a theme with my students?

II.   How does theme development lead to integration of all subject matter? What are the steps to developing this integration?

III.   How do I use student choice to motivate students to develop their own ideas?

I. What is a theme? How do I develop the idea of a theme with my students?

Galileo once said, "You can teach a man or woman nothing. You can only help him/her discover it within himself/herself." This is a good saying to keep in mind as we explore the idea of developing themes. Whatever steps we follow, inevitably it is the children's desire to learn that will determine the success of your theme.

The First Theme of the Year

Procedure:

A.   Study the following documents before beginning with your children.

    1.   State department curriculum guide for your area and discipline

    2.   District course of study-action plan or vision statement

    3.   Individual school improvement plan or other document that states and describes goals and objectives

    4.   Current research in the field

B.   Follow reflective inquiry (Barr, Barth, & Shermis, 1977)[2] to create or discover a problem to solve. Be sure your children practice the following:

    1.   Encoding information: Understanding the difference between relevant and irrelevant information in solving a problem.

    2.   Combining information: Putting something previously known or learned together with new information.

    3.   Comparing problems: Knowing how to look for similarities or differences in previously encountered problems and to use already learned skills and concepts.

C.   Ryan and Ellis (1974)[3] describe the process as:

    1.   Recognizing a problem

    2.   Selecting appropriate data sources

     3. Processing data

     4. Making inferences from data

D. When introducing the theme, consider using:

     1. A book in the subject/concept area you're discussing. For example, you could read one of the *Eyewitness* books for either science or social studies. There are a range of books in this series on many subjects. (See Chapter 5 for lists of the books.)

     2. Children's interests can be reflected in things they bring from home such as seashells, bears, baseball cards, and so forth. Then consider questions that might suggest a theme. Using the seashells you might ask, "Where do they come from? What other creatures might live in that body of water?" Then lead to an exploration of sea creatures, oceans, tides, and currents. Your children will suggest many ideas for themes if motivated in this manner.

     3. Use an artifact that you've acquired from traveling or have in your school or public library or local museum (such as brass scales from Italy, a mask from Central America, American Indian objects, and so on). This can open up the door to many questions and suggestions for themes such as Cultures from Around the World or the World as a Community, or other such examples.

E. Consider the following when planning your thematic units:

     1. Select a topic or theme that is both developmentally appropriate and follows the children's needs and interests.

     2. Brainstorm ideas with students by:

        a. Discussions

        b. Webbing/mapping

        c. Illustrating

        d. Listing ideas/concepts

        e. Doing a strategy such as K.W.L. to determine a starting point

        f. Deciding main concept and theme title to be developed

     3. Be sure students understand necessity to study the topic and its relevance to their lives.

     4. Determine experiences and activities to facilitate learning/problem solving.

     5. Gather and plan resources—books, articles, field trips, interviews, guest speakers, letters of inquiry.

     6. Organize rooms in centers or set up certain areas for resources.

     7. Consult school and public librarians, media specialists, museum personnel, art and music teachers, and others.

8. Inform school staff, principal, and parents of your topic. They will contribute help, ideas, and suggestions.

9. Teach any skills necessary such as a particular writing format, note taking, report writing, or research and reference skills.

10. Provide a large block of time for students to read and answer questions determined during the webbing, discussion, or KWL stage.

11. Establish many types of groupings to work on the theme such as individuals, partners, small group, and whole class.

12. Promote collaboration, choice, and create varied formats for study.

13. Model strategies as the need arises in the form of mini-lessons such as realizing many students are having difficulty with grammar. Stop and teach some rules of grammar and provide samples.

14. Encourage students to proceed on their own, following leads, discovering facts, investigating, collecting data, problem solving, revising, rethinking, and so forth.

F. Teacher's Role

1. Model and encourage authentic language for meaningful purposes.

2. Use cooperative learning style but also encourage individuals to work on their own. Use pairs, small groups and whole class lessons.

3. Foster risk taking and problem solving.

4. Provide activities and projects so children can experience integrating Speaking, Listening, Reading, and Writing into all the curricular areas.

5. Foster choice and ownership of the activities. Encourage autonomy and control of their own learning.

6. Provide feedback that facilitates self-regulation and independent learning.

G. Students' Role

1. Demonstrate responsibility for their learning by constructing their own knowledge.

2. Be risk takers by generating and testing hypotheses.

3. Use authentic language; read and write constantly to create their own unique style.

4. Integrate Speaking, Listening, Reading, and Writing into all activities and projects.

5. Create choices and ownership in whatever they do.

6. Interact and cooperate/collaborate with peers and teachers.

7. Use as many sources for learning as possible. (Don't forget interviewing people for authenticity of learning.)

8. Evaluate self and modify theories and concepts by getting feedback from peers and teachers.

II. How does theme development lead to integration of all subject matter? What are the steps to developing this integration?

When planning an integrated unit some teachers prefer to do most of the planning themselves. However, planning should be done collaboratively with the students to be sure they are given a voice and consequently will want to share in ownership of the unit or theme. Try some of the following ways to integrate your unit.

A. Consider four or five areas or themes to explore. Let the students pick the one they want to pursue.

B. Think about your theme and ways it could be incorporated in Math, Social Studies, and Science. (Remember that the language arts areas of Reading, Writing, Spelling, and English are inherent in any theme as you will be doing all of these things as you develop the theme.)

C. Web your ideas with the children to include suggestions for concept development in all curriculum areas.

D. Model all strategies/skills you want students to utilize.

E. Gather your materials and sources. Keep in mind that students themselves will do this as they progress.

F. Use a book, film, artifact, or guest speaker to motivate interest.

G. Pick groups to investigate each concept. Let the students choose which ones to pursue and what kind of grouping they prefer. It may be that some students prefer to investigate some idea on their own.

H. Establish blocks of time to work on theme.

I. Discuss rules of behavior and self-evaluation techniques and strategies.

J. Organize room and send students into areas or centers of the room that have pens, pencils, paper, poster boards, markers, staplers, rulers, and other supplies already there.

III. How do I use student choice to motivate students to develop their own ideas?

Whenever you present concepts to develop to your students you need to consider choice. You won't have complete choice at first, but limited in the sense that you give choices within parameters.

Let us consider a case in point to fully understand limited choices. We will take a particular theme, follow the steps outlined above, and then see what the choices may be and how to encourage those choices.

FIGURE 4–1 Teaching the Theme "Growing with Food" Across the Curriculum

Materials: nutritional labels, ingredients, cooking utensils, menus, fake money, recipes, manipulatives

Resources: Stone Soup, The M&M's Counting Book, The Hungry Little Boy, grocery store

Math
- counting and adding calories
- measurement to Stone Soup
- following recipes and combining ingredients
- ordering and paying for the food
- nutrition labels/ multiplication

Resources: encyclopedias, reference materials, What Happens to a Hamburger, posters

Science
- trace bodies and draw in digestive system
- roles and function of digestive system
- grow food in class

Materials: large paper, markers, scissors, tape, seeds, soil, water, data entry sheets

Resources: magazines, cookbooks

Art
- collages of pictures of food
- making food out of art supplies
- make desserts and other foods for show

Materials: posterboard, glue, scissors, playdough, clay, dessert ingredients

Social Studies
- map booklets of certain countries and which foods they produce
- What food is important in your culture?
- discuss food shortages in different parts of the world and see how we can help them

Resources: encyclopedias, atlases, cookbooks, consumer labels, community members

Materials: construction paper, stapler, crayons

Growing with Food

Music
- sound production
- make your own instrument with food
- glass rubbing

Materials: various containers, liquids, dry foods, glasses

Physical Education
- counting calories burned while exercising
- monitoring the energy used and the way that one feels during exercise

Materials: exercise machine with device to count calories, data entry sheet

Resources: community member, references for metabolism

Literature
- Booklet of what foods you would like to fall from the sky.
- write a play or story about your favorite food
- write a poem in a food's perspective

Resources: Cloudy with a Chance of Meatballs

Materials: paper, writing utensils, imagination, crayons, markers, etc.

66

FIGURE 4–2 Teaching the Theme "Strange and Exciting Creatures" Across the Curriculum

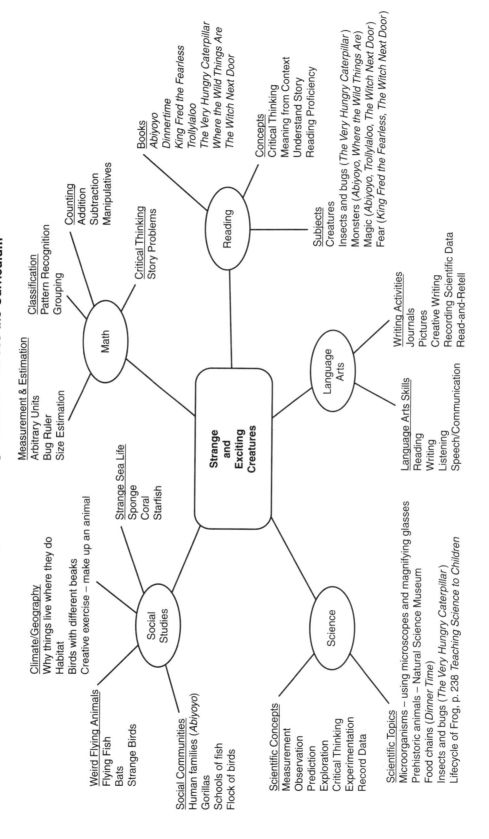

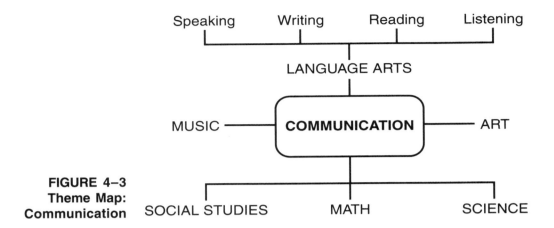

FIGURE 4–3
Theme Map:
Communication

Let's say we're going to develop a theme around the idea or concept of "Communication" because it fits into your science curriculum and is in your grade level guide. You would begin, as we said, by discussing the theme and seeing how it could be incorporated into all the subject areas.

Once you decided the webbing or mapping, you could then utilize choice. You could ask the students to pick a subject area in the map you've created and explore what to study. You could let them choose members of their group. It would be their responsibility to figure out how and what resources to use in examining the subject. (Of course it would depend on the grade level. You would need to provide more direction to the younger students. *But* you could still give them choices within the parameters *you* choose.)

When each group has reported back to the class, it would then be time to give choices again. This time they could choose to go on with the subject area they've explored for resources or the whole class could study one subject area at a time. If this is the course you take, the children would still work in groups or alone and examine one subtopic within the subject area. Let's say you've chosen science to work on together. Suppose one subtopic is *talking* or *sound*. If you had chosen this area to explore, you might want to again make a web with sound as the main topic in the center.

Once you have distributed the subject areas or subtopics within them, you then need to determine blocks of time to do the research. You could plan on working the whole day if the decision was to do all the subjects. If it was examining one subject at a time, you would just set aside maybe two blocks of time. Or another idea is to plan to pursue other areas within the theme but do it together with the teacher planning and executing it. So your day might look like this.

If you continue to ask students for input in everything you do, they will take ownership and become more and more independent. If, however, you give them too much independence too soon, you will discourage them from wanting to become independent. It has to come in stages and is dependent upon grade level as well. It is better to err on the side of slowly relinquishing responsibility than to expect too much too soon.

Time	Monday	Tuesday	Wednesday	Thursday	Friday
8:45			Consistent Morning Exercises		
9:05	Language Arts		Theme Reading/Writing		Art/Gym
10:45			Recess		
11:05	Science/Social Studies		Theme Research/Note Taking		
12:15			Lunch/Recess		
12:50	Math-Theme Related			Music/Library	
2:05			Theme Related Activities		
3:10			Dismissal		

Note: All these times are subject, of course, to your specific school schedules and specials (art, music, gym, and so on). The important issue is integrating your theme into all your curriculum. You will be able eventually to not even label your blocks of your time as subjects, but rather as simply blocks of time to develop your theme that will include many opportunities to do math/social studies/science and include lots of reading/writing and research. It takes time to learn what skills, concepts, and ideas you need to teach for your particular grade level. Once you are familiar with what's expected of you, you can start using your own way to teach them.

TABLE 4–1 Weekly Schedule— Theme Development

School Year Progression

Teacher	Student / Teacher	Student
Modeling	*Direct Teaching/ Learning*	*Student-Led and Developed*
*Strategies	*Concepts	*Strategies
*Cooperative Learning	*Skills *Conferencing	*Projects *Presentations
*Theme Development	*Integration of Subject Matter	*Conferences *Celebrations of Learning
*Use of Materials Metacognition	*Development of Partnerships— Business/Community	*Business/ Community Partnerships

*This progression moves along according to individual classes, teachers, and scheduling. There is no set time for any phase of the development.

TABLE 4–2 Releasing Responsibility for Learning from Teacher to Student

Topic

K	W	L
What we know	What we want to know	What we learned and still want to learn

Source: Ogle, Donna. 1986. "The K.W.L.: A teaching model that develops active reading of expository text." *The Reading Teacher,* 39, pp. 564–576.

TABLE 4–3 K.W.L. Strategy Sheet

ENDNOTES

1. Johnson et al. "Effect of Cooperative, Competitive and Individualistic Goal Structures on Achievement: A Meta-Analysis," *Psychological Bulletin* 89 (1981): 4762.

2. R. Barr, J. Barth, and S. S. Shermis, *Defining Social Studies*. Bulletin 51 (Washington, DC: National Council for the Social Studies, 1977).

3. F. Ryan and A. Ellis, *Instructional Implications of Inquiry* (Englewood Cliffs, NJ: Prentice Hall, 1974).

REFERENCES

Barr, R.; Barth, J.; and Shermis, S. S. *Defining Social Studies*. Bulletin 51. Washington, DC: National Council for the Social Studies, 1977.

Brozo, William, and Simpson, Michele. *Readers, Teachers, Learners: Expanding Literacy in Secondary Schools*. 2nd ed. Englewood Cliffs, NJ: Prentice Hall.

Fairfax County Public Schools. *Elementary Writing Guide*. Writing Across the Curriculum Tape 4. Fairfax County, VA, 1987. Reprinted by permission.

Pappas, Christine C.; Kiefer, Barbara Z.; and Levstik, Linda S. *An Integrated Language Perspective in the Elementary School: Theory into Action*. White Plains, NY: Longman, 1990.

Routman, Regie. *Invitations: Changing as Teachers and Learners K–12*. Toronto, Canada: Irwin; Portsmouth, NH: Heinemann, 1991, 235–236; 276–293.

Ryan, F.; and Ellis, A. *Instructional Implications of Inquiry*. Englewood Cliffs, NJ: Prentice Hall, 1974.

Tchudi, Susan. *Integrated Language Arts in the Elementary School*. Belmont, CA: Wadsworth Publishing Co., 1994.

CHAPTER 5

Creating a Classroom Library

PHILOSOPHY

Establishing a comprehensive classroom library is an essential component for developing independent learners. You must provide a variety of books for all the activities that occur in your classroom. When you model strategies, you need to have an array of books from which to choose to illustrate that particular strategy. You also need a variety of books for interest, ability, and for self-selected reading. It's important to have practice or basal readers for many different independent reading levels. If you teach a second grade, you need readers from first grade and third or fourth grade as well.

Nonfiction books for study or theme development in Science and Social Studies are good to have available. Reference books are also important. At the very least, you need dictionaries, thesauruses, and a set of encyclopedias.

The current libraries and media-centers in school buildings, and public libraries in communities, provide many books and references that you need for teaching. You should get books for pleasure reading, projects, unit or theme, and resources on a regular basis. But it is important to have some in your room, too.

There are many ways you can collect books for your classroom library. Listed below are the ways I've collected them over the years.

1. Book clubs such as Scholastic, Trumpet, and Troll (addresses at end of chapter)

2. Used book stores—check Yellow Pages

3. Book stores with discounted sales to teachers—check Yellow Pages and call

4. Parents, A.A.U.W., or other organizations that have sales

5. Garage and estate sales

6. Used book fair in your school (see Chapter 3 for details)

7. Book distributors—check Yellow Pages

8. Relatives (especially those with grown children)

You might consider collecting the following genres. (See end of chapter for lists of books in each category.)

Poetry

Early Grades (K–2)
1. Nursery rhymes
2. Nonsense verse
3. Rhymes
4. Contemporary poetry

Middle Grades (3–6)
1. Contemporary poetry (more sophisticated)
2. Limericks
3. Narratives
4. Ballads

Drama

Plays of any kind that fit grade level or any good literature that lends itself to drama

Fiction

Early Grades
1. Fairy tales
2. Folktales
3. Cartoons
4. Picture books
5. Award-winning contemporary fiction
6. Mysteries

Middle Grades
1. Fables
2. Tall tales
3. Myths and legends
4. Science fiction
5. Award-winning contemporary fiction
6. Mysteries
7. Historical fiction

Nonfiction

Early Grades

    1. Informational books (Science, Social Studies)

    2. ABC books

    3. Magazines

    4. Textbooks

Middle Grades

    1. Biographies/Autobiographies

    2. Textbooks

    3. Informational books

    4. Magazines

    5. Reference books

    6. Newspapers

The following American Library Association Awards, Honors, and Book Lists are available to you by writing to the American Library Association, 50 East Huron Street, Chicago, Illinois 60611 (Telephone: 312-280-2153). The awards are:

1. *BBYA—Best Books for Young Adults.* Annual selection of books with appeal to ages 12–18. (YALSA)

2. *Caldecott Honor Books.* Exceptional picture books of the year. (ALSC)

3. *Caldecott Medal.* Best picture book of the year. (ALSC)

4. *Coretta Scott King Award.* Yearly recognition of Black author and illustrator for inspirational or educational contribution. (SRRT)

5. *Newbery Honor Book.* One of the year's exceptional works of literature for children published in the United States. (ALSC)

6. *Newbery Medal.* The year's most distinguished work of literature published in the United States.

7. *Batchelder Award.* The year's most outstanding children's book originally printed in another language. (ALSC)

8. *Nothing But the Best.* Book titles, 1968–1988.

LEARNING PRINCIPLES

This chapter will relate to:

Principle 3—*The Construction of Knowledge.* The learner organizes information in ways that associate and link new information with existing knowledge in memory in uniquely meaningful ways.

Principle 12—*Cognitive Filters*. Personal thoughts, beliefs, and understandings resulting from prior learning and unique interpretations become each individual's basis for constructing reality and interpreting life experiences.

The questions discussed in this chapter are:

I. What are predictable books? How can I use them to teach strategies in the early grades?

II. What are the uses of Big Books (K–2)?

III. What kinds of books should I have for intermediate grades and how can I use them for instruction?

IV. What kinds of books do I need for multicultural learning?

V. What kinds of informational texts do I need? How do I use them?

VI. What about classic literature, poetry, plays, choral readings? How do I help students to enjoy this literature?

I. What are predictable books? How can I use them to teach strategies in the early grades?

A. There are several types of books that would qualify as predictable books. They are books that are easy to read and have parts in them that are repeated over and over. Or they are books with story lines done in rhyme. Many books are folktales told over and over or familiar fairy tales.

They are called predictable because they have some of the following features that allow young children in particular to cope with the text. They include common story patterns or story grammar, repetition of story structure or vocabulary (or both), rhythm, and rhyme.

Children enjoy saying the familiar parts aloud. And even if you don't ask them to respond, they will anyway. Through this repetition and participation, children learn a lot about words and sounds that letters make. This is especially true in the case of rhyming words. Children learn patterns in words and begin to see multiple words that can be made by using vowel patterns or ending patterns that can easily be changed by adding different beginning sounds. In fact this is an excellent extended lesson after children have read these predictable books. The vowel patterns in the Dr. Seuss books are a good example of this.

1. For example, *The Cat in the Hat*

By using the vowel pattern "-at" children can make a lot of words. A good lesson after reading the story might be to find all the words with the vowel pattern "-at" and see if you can think of any more. Have your children work in pairs and see how many words they can find and make.

cat	rat	flat
hat	fat	brat
bat	pat	slat
sat	vat	
mat		

2. Then you might have them use some words they made to make up a story, like Dr. Seuss does.

3. It's also good for teaching flexible sounding of letters and vowel patterns by trying different ones.

Some books with predictable patterns are fairy tales such as *Sleeping Beauty, Cinderella, Snow White and the Seven Dwarfs, Little Red Riding Hood, The Magic Fish*, and others.

You might read books that illustrate *cause and effect* such as *Noisy Nora, The Rose in My Garden*, and *Are You My Mother?* To help students understand this concept you might want to write *cause and effect* on some chart paper and then discuss some cause and effect issues that are relevant to your students' life. If you don't do your homework—you don't learn. You don't have lunch money—you don't get lunch. You lose your house key—you can't get in the house, and so forth.

Another type of predictable story is the one that includes a series of *sequential events* such as those evident in *The Little Red Hen, The Gingerbread Man, I Know an Old Lady, Old MacDonald, Bunches and Bunches of Bunnies*, and so on.

You can also do a relevant lesson that your children can connect to their lives. You can list sequential activities all the children experience every day. Get up in the morning, wash their face, brush their teeth, comb their hair, get dressed, eat breakfast, go to school. You can discuss beginning, middle, and end of sequences, books and so forth. First, next, and last is another sequence to teach.

Besides constructing lists and their own stories, children can also act out these stories. Children love drama and these stories lend themselves to wonderful role-playing.

Following is a list of predictable books for children. You should try to get as many as you can.

Are You My Mother?

Bremen-Town Musicians

Brown Bear, Brown Bear, What Do You See?

Bunches and Bunches of Bunnies

Cats and Mice

Clifford's Family

Doctor DeSoto

Doctor Seuss books (such as *The Cat in the Hat, Green Eggs and Ham*)

Frog and Toad books (several titles)

Henny Penny

I Know an Old Lady

I Went Walking

Mother Goose Nursery Rhymes

Noisy Nora

On Market Street

Over in the Meadow

Stone Soup

The Elves and the Shoemaker

The Emperor's New Clothes

The Gingerbread Man

The Little Red Hen

The Magic Fish

The Three Bears

The Three Billy Goats Gruff

The Three Blind Mice

The Very Hungry Caterpillar

Where Have You Been?

Who's in the Shed?

B. Teaching strategies using predictable books

1. There are many strategies you can model using predictable books. Let's take the book *I Went Walking* and see what strategies you could use. This book takes the children on a walk with an unusual looking little boy who adds one animal after another as he walks along. It lends itself to teaching *prediction* as each page gives a hint (a tail or part of an animal) to help the children guess what's coming next. Each page starts with the repeating sentence, "I went walking and what did I see? I saw a little _____ looking at me." Because of the patterning and use of rhyming, it also lends itself to teaching *sequencing* and *rhyming words*. So an extended lesson could include:

   a. Making lists of the rhyming words; using the vowel pattern and making more words.

   b. Discussing sequencing and using cartoons, story strips with sentences out of order to put in sequence, pictures of the story to put in order, and so on.

   c. Making up another story that lists things in sequence. This could be a class book or you could have the children choose partners or small groups and produce a story on their own.

2. For each book you use, decide on a strategy that is appropriate. The following strategies could be used.

    a. Teaching prediction and prior knowledge—using pictures, title, and experiences

    b. Teaching sequencing

    c. Teaching rhyming words

    d. D.R.T.A. (Direct Reading Thinking Activity)

    e. Story structure—events of the story in order

    f. Story grammar—characters, setting, problems, events, ending

II. What are the uses of Big Books (K–2)?

Big Books are basically used to help children learn to read more quickly. They can also be used for group practice of oral reading, choral, and echo reading as well as rehearsal for reading the book individually. It's a good way to do word study and guided reading as the children are more apt to be paying close attention to the reading because of the size of the book and close proximity to the teacher.

There are necessary steps to follow when reading Big Books. It is essential that you take the time to organize and plan your presentation. Don't try and do too much in one day. Spread your presentation and extended lessons over three or four days and do it in small groups of eight or ten children. The following activities can be planned and executed over the three to four days you will share the book.

A. *Read many big books and choose a book* that is appropriate for your children. Both grade and interest level need to be considered.

B. *Decide on the strategies* you will model. (Don't do too many for one book, just one or two.)

C. The first day you need to:

    1. *Introduce the book* by holding it up and discussing the cover: title, picture, and so on.

    2. *Call on prior knowledge* of your students to discuss what has happened to them or what they've heard about or seen on TV that remind them of the picture or theme.

    3. *List their ideas, discussion points, experiences, and so forth* on chart paper or board.

    4. *Discuss author, illustrator* (whether they're familiar)

    5. *Explain publisher, copyright, and dedication* so they become familiar with the workings of books.

    6. *Ask what do you think this story will be about? (Prediction)* List what they say on chart paper or board. (Save.)

D. The second day:

1. *Read the book aloud* with enthusiasm, expression, and drama

2. *Emphasize patterns, rhyming words, predictable parts, repetitions, and so on.*

3. *Let your children read aloud* the repetitious, rhyming words with you, but don't stop for comments on this first reading as it interferes with the flow of the storyline.

4. *Discuss their lists of ideas, predictions, and other thoughts,* seeing how many are represented in the story.

5. *Praise lavishly* when their ideas or concepts match the ones in the story. Be flexible in determining their matches. (Use your chart paper/board to put checks on matches.)

6. *Let the children express opinions and reflect on the story freely.* Take time for this: children learn from each other during discussions and they also confirm their thinking.

E. The third day:

1. *Reread the book* stopping for comments, asking questions, letting children ask questions, examining pictures, and so on.

2. *Have children answer questions, raise points themselves.* Try not to talk too much. Let them help each other.

3. *Take time to carefully reread each page letting children tell their differing opinions, ideas, and so forth.* Go over print to confirm or clarify points.

4. *Allow for differing opinions not voicing what you think is correct.* They need to think about *their* memories, ideas, books *they've* read with similar ideas, and so on. Only guide and watch for indications they've exhausted ideas or are getting off the subject.

5. *Be observant.* Think about how much they understand, how they're expressing opinions, ideas, and thoughts. Check their language, interpretations, experiences. Make notes after the session.

6. *Give an extended lesson* to those finishing the reading as you work with the next group. They could draw pictures of the story in sequence, draw one picture, write their impression of the story, retell it in their own words, write a story that is similar, and so forth.

F. The fourth day:

1. *Have the children pick partners and reread the story* together by using the smaller versions of the big books.

2. *Choose small groups to reread the story* choosing a student to be teacher to mediate the reading.

3. *Children can use the small books to:*

a. practice reading vocabulary

b. learn how to ask and answer questions

c. act them out making a play or skit

d. tape-record them reading

e. read to older students, parents, principal, and others

f. do word study—looking for words starting with particular letters, blends, similar meanings, and so on

g. write their own books or stories using plots and characters that are similar

h. make cloze passages to evaluate individual children's comprehension of main ideas or points in the story. (Use any one of the types of cloze exercises mentioned in Chapter 2.)

G. Keep in mind that big books are not simply oversized books but must be books of high-quality literature. Look for books that use language well, tell an interesting story, and contain enticing illustrations.

Consider some of the following:

Aliki, *My Five Senses*

Asch, *Happy Birthday Moon*

Baker, *Where the Forest Meets the Sea*

Baker, *Who Is the Beast?*

Bang, *Ten, Nine, Eight*

Barbour, *Little Nino's Pizzeria*

Barton, *Dinosaurs, Dinosaurs*

Bridwell, *Clifford's Family*

Brown and Bond, *Big Red Barn*

Brown, *A Dark, Dark Tale*

Cole, *The Magic School Bus*

Dodds, *Wheel Away*

Ehlert, *Growing Veg Soup*

Fox, *Hattie and the Fox*

Fox, *Night Noises*

Freeman, *Corduroy*

Ginsburg, *Across the Stream*

Heller, *Kites Sail High*

Hutchins, *Good Night Owl*

Hutchins, *The Surprise Party*

Kellogg, *Pinkerton, Behave!*

Kraus, *Whose Mouse Are You?*

Mayer, *There's a Nightmare in My Closet*

Martin, *The Happy Hippopotami*

McCloskey, *Make Way for Ducklings*

Most, *The Cow That Went Oink*

Numeroff, *If You Give a Mouse a Cookie*

Numeroff, *If You Give a Mouse a Muffin*

Noble, *The Day Jimmy's Boa Ate the Wash*

Reid, *Sing a Song of Mother Goose*

Rye, *Look, What Do You See?*

Tanner, *Nicki's Walk*

Walsh, *Mouse Paint*

Wells, *Morris's Disappearing Bag*

Williams, *I Went Walking*

Wood, *The Napping House*

These books can be purchased in different ways: through basal reading programs, book clubs, and directly from publishers. You need to ask your school or public librarian where to purchase some. Or just borrow them from their collections. Most of the big books are used in kindergarten through second-grade classrooms. But, there are some that are appealing to third or fourth graders. And there are many being planned in the nonfiction area that will have a wide range of interests for many grade levels. Keep up to date by checking with your librarians and visiting book stores. Many book clubs are now selling them and if you have Scholastic, Troll, or Trumpet in your school, check to see what they offer.

III. What kinds of books should I have for intermediate grades and how can I use them for instruction?

At about third- or fourth-grade level, children want to start reading what they refer to as "chapter" books. There are wonderful novels for children ages 8 to 12 or so that keep their interest growing page after page. Most teachers now are teaching from novels that are familiar and are considered high-quality literature such as *Anne of Green Gables, Borrowed Children, Bridge to Terabithia*, all the Encyclopedia Brown books (such as *Encyclopedia Brown and the Case of the Disgusting Sneakers*, and others), *Fudge-a-Mania*, and so on. At the beginning of the year, it is important to select novels to read together. I would again select some books you would like to have your students read (with multiple copies available) and some they pick to read themselves.

A. After you've developed this list, it is important to:

1. Read each book yourself.

2. Decide on strategies you will teach or model.

3. Determine the method of reading the books with the children. You could use:

   a. Partner reading

   b. Teacher reading

   c. Small group reading

   d. Whole class reading

4. Decide on extended lessons using the first novel you'll read. The class will determine the extended lessons on the rest of the books.

B. How do I use them for instruction?

   After you've picked the first novel the students will read, you need to directly teach it. This will help the students understand and practice how to proceed with the additional novels you'll read together.

   It's a good strategy to tell them a little about each novel to spark interest. Say, for example, you've decided to include *Borrowed Children* on your list. You would need to do the following:

1. Hold up the book and discuss the writer. Tell a little about her or him.

2. Discuss when the novel was written. (There will be some classic books that you can discuss. Children need to know why some books are read generation after generation.)

3. Tell a little about the book:

   When her mother is bedridden, twelve-year-old Amanda takes over. Her mother has just had a baby and Amanda has to do everything—cook meals, wash clothes, feed, and care for the baby Willie and her mom. She also has to stay out of school. This novel takes place in Kentucky in the 1930s and life is very hard during the Depression. Dad works at a timber mill and is away all week. By the time her mom is better Amanda wishes she lived anywhere but where she does live. So when her grandparents write to invite her to come to Memphis, she jumps at the chance. It's so nice to be in the big city and enjoy all the wonderful things to do. Things happen, however, that make her realize other people's lives aren't always what they seem, and she begins to miss the warmth of her own family.

4. Read the book aloud with discussion before to preview and after to reflect.

5. During or after the reading of the book, consider using extended lessons.

a. Learn about the Depression. Have children read about it and interview folks who lived through the Depression. Make tapes or reports on their histories.

b. Discuss jobs then and now. How has the country changed?

c. Discuss families now and then. How are they different?

d. Reflect on the universal theme "The Grass is Always Greener on the Other Side of the Fence." Relate it to your students' lives. What do they wish was different in their own lives? What are they thankful for?

e. Do murals, collages, or some kind of art work.

f. Listen to country music. Compose a song or poem.

g. Get books on Kentucky and have a small group report on it.

When you have finished the first novel (four to five weeks) then pick another to read that you have discussed. (Remember to give a synopsis of all the books on the list.)

The next book should be not only picked by your students, but they should determine the way in which they will read it. You will serve as a "coach" and simply guide them and work with individual children or groups of children that experience difficulty either with the reading of the book or in understanding it. It is important to remember to vary the approach when teaching novels so that you keep interest and alleviate boredom. You might do whole group lessons in grammar, cause and effect, drawing inferences, conclusions, or any other concepts or skills listed in your curriculum guide.

That's why it's important to study your guides or outcomes at the beginning of the year so you can weave them into your teaching and guiding of lessons. It is important, when you use novels, that you continually evaluate your students' progress. Give periodic writing assignments, quizzes, or any other form of reflection you consider important, to see if your students are understanding the concepts/skills being presented.

IV. What kinds of books do I need for multicultural learning?

When you are considering the books you will read, be sure to include some multicultural ones. Not only is it important for your children to respect and become tolerant of those who are different from themselves, but it is also rewarding to explore the countries, religions, customs, and so forth that are evident in these differences. When you consider themes, there are always ways to weave in some different cultures and customs.

One book that comes to mind is the book *Two Short and One Long*. This is a story of two boys from Norway. Their friendship is tested when an Afghan refugee comes to their school. There are violent and intense scenes that involve anti-racist messages. It tells how the children and their parents reassess their beliefs, values, and behavior. It is also filled with interesting adventures with which children ages nine to twelve can relate.

Use the list at the end of the chapter and choose a few to explore with your children.

V. What kinds of informational texts do I need? How do I use them?

    A. You will need books for the themes that you pick at the beginning of the year. But you also need reference books as well so that children can pursue their own interests and look up facts as needed.

        I would suggest the following books as essential components of a classroom library (along with books borrowed from other libraries in school or in your community).

        1. *A set of encyclopedias*—You can get these at estate sales, library sales (they sometimes sell their old sets), from friends, relatives with grown children, and others. Be sure however, that they're not older than five years. Otherwise the information is apt to be incorrect. You always need to be cognizant of this.

        2. *Books on animals, science, social studies,* and other topics—whatever nonfiction books you can lay your hands on. Again look at book sales, estate sales, and library sales for your purchases. And don't be too picky. There are so many subject areas in which your students are interested that you can't make too many mistakes. Just be sure the books are not too old. Some books, of course, are ageless because they're simply factual books that don't change. (See some listed at the end of the chapter.)

        3. *Magazines* such as *Boys' Life, Calliope, Clavier's Piano Explorer, Cobblestone,* to name a few. These magazines will have current articles regarding hobbies, world events, sports, explorers, famous battles, television, and other subjects. It's important to know your children's interest when making the choice. Get some copies from the library and peruse them. (See list at the end of the chapter.)

        4. *Newspapers*—Subscribe to a good daily newspaper or use one that comes to your school. (I always preferred to have my own copy because we always cut it up.) Have a current events time each day to discuss the newspaper and world and local events.

    B. How do I use them?

        1. You need to have *encyclopedias* for the following activities:

            a. As a reference for the things that come up each day as children are free to explore their world.

            b. As a teaching tool to show them over and over how to do research and use a reference book correctly.

            c. For simple perusing. There are many children who love to just look over encyclopedias.

        2. You need *books* for all the themes you'll explore.

      a. For research into various aspects of your theme.

      b. For you to read to your students for expediency at times.

      c. For extended lessons in reading/writing.

3. *Magazines* are useful because of the following reasons:

      a. Children often decide to pursue something on their own.

      b. Hobbies that children enjoy reading about.

      c. Current information in more depth than in newspapers.

      d. Theme development in a wide variety of areas.

4. *Newspapers* are useful because you often need up-to-the-minute information for reports or discussions and to learn about how newspapers are written, produced, and printed.

VI. What about classic literature, poetry, plays, choral readings? How do I help students to enjoy this literature?

I always felt that I should introduce my students to classic literature and poetry and plays. The way I did this was to write to the American Library Association that I mentioned at the beginning of the chapter. I asked them to send me a list of fiction books and poetry that were considered classics for the interest level of my age students. Or I sometimes went to the local library and spoke to the librarian in charge that would know about the books and poetry in that library.

After looking over the list and reading some of the books, I would make my decision based on my particular classes' interests and on themes that we were going to study. I also picked a few that I really liked and thought the children might enjoy that were not necessarily interest-level or theme-related but just plain interesting and well written. (See a list at the end of the chapter).

I also thought that plays and choral reading were good for my students to develop poise and to help with self-esteem. So, I picked some after looking over those available at the libraries. Again, you can sometimes develop a nice collection of plays and choral reading pieces by going to library sales, or book sales of some kind.

TABLE 5–1
ABC Books

Aardvarks, Disembark. Jonas, Ann.
Alligator Arrived with Apples: A Potluck Alphabet Feast. Dragonwagon, Crescent
Alphabatics. MacDonald, Suse.
Beach Ball. Sis, Peter.
Chicka, Chicka, Boom, Boom. Martin, Bill and John Archambault.
Eating the Alphabet: Fruits and Vegetables from A to Z. Ehlert, Lois.
The Handmade Alphabet. Rankin, Laura.
I Can Be the Alphabet. Bonini, Marinella.
If There Were Dreams to Sell. Laliki, Barbara.
Pigs from A to Z. Geisert, Arthur.

Compton's Encyclopedia. Encyclopedia Brittanica. 1992.
New Book of Knowledge. Grolier. 1992.
World Book. World Book. 1992.

Early Grades

American Heritage First Dictionary. Houghton Mifflin. 1986.
Macmillan First Dictionary. Macmillan. 1990.
Words for New Readers. Scott, Foresman. 1990.
My First Dictionary. Scott, Foresman, 1990.

Intermediate Grades

**TABLE 5–2
Encyclopedias
and Dictionaries**

The American Heritage Children's Dictionary. Houghton Mifflin. 1986.
Macmillan Dictionary for Children. Macmillan. 1989.
Thorndike-Barnhart Children's Dictionary. Scott, Foresman. 1988.
Webster's Elementary Dictionary. Merriam-Webster. 1986.
Webster's New World Children's Dictionary. Simon and Schuster. 1991.

Annotated Bibliography of Children's Books (updated each year). 1995 ed. by P. Genick. 623 Lakeside Drive, Waterford, MI 48328. (810) 682-2937.

Booklinks (bimonthly September to May). American Library Association. 50 East Huron Street, Chicago, IL 60611.

Choosing Books for Children: A Common Sense Guide. Betsy Hearne. Delacorte/Delta. 1990 rev. ed.

The New Read-Aloud Handbook. James Trelease. Penguin. 1989 rev. ed.

**TABLE 5–3
Book Lists**

The New York Times Parent's Guide to the Best Books for Children. Eden Ross Lipson. Times Books/Random House. 1991 rev. ed.

TABLE 5–4 Magazines

Early Grades

Boomerang
Listen and Learn
  Home Education
123 Townsend Street,
  Suite 636
San Francisco, CA 94107
	Cricket
	315 Fifth Street
	Peru, IL 61354
		Hidden Pictures
		  Magazine
		2300 W. Fifth Avenue
		PO Box 269
		Columbus, OH 43216
			Hopscotch, The Magazine
			  for Girls
			PO Box 1292
			Satatoga Springs, NY
			  12866

Kid City, For Graduates
  of Sesame Street
1 Lincoln Plaza
New York, NY 10023
	Kids Discover
	170 Fifth Avenue
	New York, NY 10010
		P3, Earth-Based
		  Magazine for Kids
		PO Box 52
		Montgomery, VT 05470
			Ranger Rick
			8925 Leesburg Pike
			Vienna, VA 22184-0001

Seedling Series: Short
  Story International
6 Sheffield Road
Great Neck, NY 11021
	Skipping Stones, A
	  Multi-Ethnic
	  Children's Forum
	80574 Hazelton Road
	Cottage Grove, OR
	  97424
		Stone Soup, The
		  Magazine by
		  Children
		Children's Art
		  Foundation
		915 Cedar Street
		Santa Cruz, CA 95060
			U.S. Kids
			245 Long Hill Road
			Middletown, CT 06457

(Cont.)

TABLE 5–4 *(Cont.)*

Early Grades

Zoobooks
Wildlife Education Ltd.
3590 Kettner Boulevard
San Diego, CA 92101

Middle Grades

Boys Life
1325 W. Walnut Hill
  Lane
PO Box 152079
Irving, TX 75015-2079
	Calliope, World
	  History for Young
	  People
	30 Grove Street
	Peterborough, NH
	  03458
		Cobblestone, The
		  History Magazine
		  for Young People
		30 Grove Street
		Peterborough, NH
		  03458
			Dolphin Log
			8440 Santa Monica
			  Boulevard
			Los Angeles, CA 90069

Faces, The Magazine
  About People
30 Grove Street
Peterborough, NH
  03458
	Kidsports
	1011 Wilson Boulevard
	Arlington, VA 22209
		National Geographic
		  World
		National Geographic
		  Society
		17th and M Street NW
		Washington, DC 20036
			Native Monthly Reader
			  (A Scholastic Newspaper
			  for Young Adults)
			Red Sun Institute
			PO Box 122
			Crestone, CO 81131

O.W.L., The Discovery
  Magazine for
  Children
The Young Naturalist
56 The Esplanade
Suite 306
Toronto, Ontario
  M5E1A7 Canada
	Plays, The Drama
	  Magazine for
	  Children
	120 Boylston Street
	Boston, MA 02116
		Sports Illustrated
		  for Kids
		Time and Life Building
		Rockefeller Center
		New York, NY
		  10020-1393
			3-2-1 Contact
			Children's Television
			  Workshop
			1 Lincoln Plaza
			New York, NY 10023

Zillions, Consumer *Reports for Kids* 101 Truman Avenue Yonkers, NY 10703			

Resources for More Magazines

Magazines for Children. Richardson, Selma. 1991 rev. ed. ALA Publishing.
Magazines for Young People. Katz, Bill and Linda Sternberg Katz. 1991. Bowker.

TABLE 5–5 Trade Books

Pre-Primer Readiness Level

Cat on the Mat. Wildsmith, Brian.
Have You Seen My Cat? Carle, Eric.
Have You Seen My Duckling? Tafuri, Nancy.
All Fall Down. Wildsmith, Brian.
Baby Says. Steptoe, John.
The Little Red House. Sawicki, N.J.
Now We Can Go. Jonas, Ann.
Toot-Toot. Wildsmith, Brian.
Brown Bear, Brown Bear, What Do You See?
   Martin, Bill.
Rain. Kalan, Robert.
Roll Over. Peek, Merle.
Spots, Feathers and Curly Tails. Tafuri, Nancy.
Five Little Ducks. Raffi.
Chick and the Duckling. Ginsburg, Mirra.

How Many Bugs in a Box? Carter, David.
I Can Build a House. Watanabe, Shigeo.
Mary Wore Her Red Dress. Peek, Merle.
Sam's Ball. Lindgren, Barbro.
Sam's Cookie. Lindgren, Barbro.
Sam's Lamp. Lindgren, Barbro.
Sam's Wagon. Lindgren, Barbro.
Flying. Crew, Donald.
It Looks Like Spilt Milk. Shaw, Chas.
The Blanket. Burmingham, John.
Five Little Monkeys Jumping on the Bed.
   Christelow, Eileen.
Henry's Busy Day. Campbell, Rod.
Oh, A Hunting We Will Go. Langstaff, John.
Where's Spot? Hill, Eric.

Primer Readiness Level

Are You There Bear? Mario, Ron.
Cat Goes Fiddle-i-Fee. Galdone, Paul.
Dear Zoo. Campbell, Rod.
Grandma and the Pirate. Lloyd, David.
Gregory's Garden. Stobbs, William.
Have You Seen the Crocodile? West, Colin.
Is Anyone Home? Maris, Ron.
Just Like Daddy. Asch, Frank.
Rosie's Walk. Hutchins, Pat.
Where's My Daddy? Watanabe, Shigeo.
Across the Stream. Ginsburg, Mirra.
Cookie's Week. Ward, Cindy and De Paola.
A Dark, Dark Tale. Brown, Ruth.
Going for a Walk. DeRegniers, B.S.
Hooray for Snail. Stadler, John.
I'm the King of the Castle. Watanabe, Shigeo.
Marmalade's Nap. Wheeler, Cindy.
Marmalade's Snowy Day. Wheeler, Cindy.
My Kitchen. Rockwell, Harlow.
Roll Over. Gerstein, Mordicai.

Thank You, Nicky! Ziefert, Harriet.
William Where Are You? Gerstein, Mordicai.
Sheep in a Jeep. Shaw, Nancy.
Ten Bears in My Bed. Mack, Stan.
Each Peach, Pear, Plum. Ahlberg, Allan and
   Ahlberg, Janet.
The Big Fat Worm. Van Laan, Nancy.
The Carrot Seed. Krauss, Ruth.
Lollipop. Watson, Wendy.
SHHH! Henkes, Kevin.
Ten Black Dots. Crews, Donald.
Three Cheers for Hippo. Stadler, John.
Three Kittens. Ginsburg, Mirra.
Titch. Hutchins, Pat.
Great Big Enormous Turnip. Oxenburg, H. Tolstoy.
If I Were a Penguin. Goenell. Heidi.
Misty's Mischief. Campbell, Rod.
One Bear All Alone. Bucknall, Caroline.
The Tool Box. Rockwell, Anne.
Two Bear Clubs. Jonas, Ann.

Level 1[2]

Building a House. Barton, Byron.
The Cake That Mack Ate. Robart, Rose.
Come Out and Play Little Mouse. Kraus, Robert.
Goodnight Moon. Brown, Margaret Wise.
I Was Walking Down the Road. Barchas, Sarah.
My Brown Bear Barney. Butler, Dorothy.
My Cat. Taylor, Judy.
Put Me in the Zoo. Lopshire, Robert.
Where Are You Going Little Mouse? Kraus, Robert.
You'll Soon Grow Into Them, Titch. Hutchins, Pat.
Airport. Barton, Byron.
Are You My Mother? Eastman, P.D.
Don't Touch. Kine, Suzy.
Fix-it. McPhail, David.
Hattie and the Fox. Fox, Mem.
The House That Jack Built. Stobbs, William.

The Napping House. Wood, Don and Wood, Audrey.
Nobody Listens to Andrew. Guildfoile, Elizabeth.
This is the Bear. Hayes, S. and Craig, H.
We're Going on a Bear Hunt. Rosen, Michael.
Who Took the Farmer's Hat. Nodset, Joan.
Who Wants One? Serfozo, Mary.
Angus and the Cat. Flack, Marjorie.
The Bear's Bicycle. McLeod, Emilie.
Benny Bakes a Cake. Rice, Eve.
Bertie the Bear. Allen, Pamela.
Chicken Licken. Bishop, Gavin.
Goodnight Owl. Hutchins, Pat.
Henny Penny. Galdone, Paul.
Just Like Everyone Else. Kuskin, Karla.
A Kiss for Little Bear. Minarik, Else H.
Leo the Late Bloomer. Kraus, Robert.

(Cont.)

TABLE 5–5   *(Cont.)*

Level 1[2]

Noisy Nora. Wells, Rosemary.
The Quilt. Jonas, Ann.
Teeny Tiny. Bennett, Jill.
The Teeny Tiny Woman. Seuling, Barbara.

There's a Nightmare in My Closet. Mayer, Mercer.
Three Billy Goat's Gruff. Brown, Marcia.
The Very Busy Spider. Carle, Eric.
The Wheels on the Bus. Kovalski, Mary Ann.

Level 2[1]

Ask Mr. Bear. Flack, Marjorie.
The Doorbell Rang. Hutchins, Pat.
The Elephant and the Bad Baby. Vipoint, Elfrida.
Funny Bones. Ahlberg, Allan and Ahlberg, Janet.
Go and Hush the Baby. Byars, Betsy.
Harold and the Purple Crayon. Johnson, Crockett.
The House That Jack Built. Peppe, Rodney.
Johnny Lion's Boots. Hurd, Edith Thatcher.
The Last Puppy. Asch, Frank.
Let's Be Enemies. Sendak, Maurice.
Little Gorilla. Bornstein, Ruth.
The Little Red Hen. Galdone, Paul.
Max. Isadora, Rachel.
Meg and Mog. Nicole, Helen.
Meg at Sea. Nicole, Helen.
Mouse Tales. Lobel, Arnold.
Stone Soup. McGovern, Ann.
There's an Alligator Under My Bed. Mayer, Mercer.
There's Something in My Attic. Mayer, Mercer.

The Three Bears. Galdone, Paul.
Trouble in the Ark. Rose, Gerald.
Where the Wild Things Are. Sendak, Maurice.
Blackboard Bear. Alexander, Martha.
The Cat in the Hat. Dr. Seuss.
Charlie Needs a Cloak. DePaola, Tomie.
Clifford the Big Red Dog. Bridwell, Norman.
George Shrinks. Joyce, William.
Jamberry. Degen, Bruce.
Jimmy Lee Did It. Cummings, Pat.
Little Bear. Minarik, Else H.
The Man Who Didn't Do His Dishes.
   Krasilovsky, Phyllis.
More Tales of Amanda Pig. Van Leeuwen, Jean.
Mrs. Higgins and Her Hen Hannah.
   Dabcovich, Lydia.
Owl at Home. Lobel, Arnold.
Sam, Who Never Forgets. Rice, Eve.
The Very Hungry Caterpillar. Carle, Eric.

Level 2[2]

Count and See. Hoban, Tana.
Growing Colors. McMillan, Bruce.
Bear Goes to Town. Browne, Anthony.
The Big Sneeze. Brown, Ruth.
Frog and Toad Are Friends. Lobel, Arnold.
Frog and Toad Together. Lobel, Arnold.
Mr. Grumpy's Motor Car. Burmingham, John.
Mr. Grumpy's Outing. Burmingham, John.
The Surprise Party. Hutchins, Pat.
The Three Billy Goats Gruff. Stevens, Janet.
What Next Baby Bear? Murphy, Jill.
You Can't Catch Me. Oppenheim, Joanne.

The Art Lesson. DePaola, Tomie.
Caps for Sale. Slobodkina, Esphyr.
Chicken Soup with Rice. Sendak, Maurice.
The Gingerbread Boy. Galdone, Paul.
Happy Birthday Moon. Asch, Frank.
I Know a Lady. Zolotow, Charlotte.
Miss Nelson Is Missing. Allard, Harry.
One-Eyed Jake. Hutchins, Pat.
The Three Little Pigs. Galdone, Paul.
Tyler Toad and the Thunder. Crowe, Robert.
Who Sank the Boat? Allen, Pamela.
The Wind Blew. Hutchins, Pat.

Level 3

Abel's Island. Steig, William.
The Accident. Carrick, Carol.
Aldo Peanut-Butter. Hurwitz, Johann.
Bobby Baseball. Kimmell-Smith, Robert.
Chronicles of Narnia. Lewis, C. S.
Fudge-a-mania. Blume, Judy.
Little Jake and Me. Jukes, Mavis.
Midnight Horse. Fleischman, Sid.

Millie Cooper 3B. Herman, Charlotte.
More Stories Julian Tells. Cameron, Ann.
Robin Hood. Hayes, Sarah.
Sarah, Plain and Tall. MacLachlin, Patricia.
   (Level 3/4)
Saying Goodbye to Grandma. Thomas, Jane Resh.
   (Level 3/4)

(Cont.)

TABLE 5-5 *(Cont.)*

Level 4

Babe, The Gallant Pig. Smith-King, Dick.
(The) Canada Geese Quilt. Warnock, Natalie Kinsey.
Dr. Dredd's Wagon of Wonder. Brittain, Bill.
Dear Mr. Henshaw. Cleary, Beverly.
Encyclopedia Brown and the Case of the Disgusting Sneakers. Sobel, Donald J.
Encyclopedia Brown: The Boy Detective in the Case of the Missing Time Capsule. Sobel, Donald J.
Facts and Fiction of Minna Pratt. MacLachlan, Patricia.
Free Fall (picture book for older students). Wiesner, David.
(The) Friendship. Taylor, Mildred.
Henry. Bawden, Nina.
Indian in the Cupboard. Banks, Lynne Reid.
Jellybean. Duder, Tessa.
The Kid in the Red Jacket. Parks, Barbara.
The Kitchen Knight: A Tale of King Arthur. Hodges, Margaret.
A Little Princess. Burnett, Frances Hodgson.

Little Tricker the Squirrel Meets Big Double the Bear. Kesey, Ken.
An Occasional Cow. Horvath, Pally.
On the Far Side of the Mountain. George, Jean Craighead.
Orp and the Chop Suey Burgers. Kline, Suzy.
The Pigs Are Flying. Rodda, Emily.
Quentin, Corn. Stolz, Mary.
The Remembering Box. Clifford, Eth.
The Secret of the Indian. Banks, Lynne Reid. (Level 4/5)
Shiloh. Naylor, Phyllis Reynolds.
Sign of the Beaver. Speare, Elizabeth. (Level 4/5)
Staying Nine. Conrad, Pam.
Sticks and Stones and Skeletons Bones. Gilson, Jamie
Strider. Cleary, Beverly.
(The) Trading Game. Slate, Alfred.
Wayside School is Falling Down. Sachar, Louis.

Level 5

Across Five Aprils. Hunt, Irene.
Afternoon of the Elves. Lisle, Jane Taylor.
Anne of Avonlea: The Continuing Story of Anne of Green Gables. Montgomery, Lucy Maud.
Anne of the Island. Montgomery, Lucy Maud.
A Blue-eyed Daisy. Rylant, Cynthia.
Bridge to Terabithia. Paterson, Katherine.
Choosing Sides. Cooper, Ilene.
Dragonwings. Yep, Lawrence.
Everywhere. Brooks, Bruce.
Josie Gambit. Shura, Mary Frances.
King of the Cloud Forests. Morpurgo, Michael.

Maniac Magee. Spinelle, Jerry.
Me, Mop and the Moondance Kid. Meyers, Walter Dean.
(The) Mermaid Summer. Hunter, Mollie.
Number the Stars. Lowry, Lois.
Rasco and the Rats of N.I.M.H. Conly, Jane Leslie.
(The) Riddle of Penncroft Farm. Jensen, Dorothea.
Rose Blanche. Innocenti, Roberto.
The Secret Life of Dilly McBean. Haas, Dorothy.
Up from Jericho Tell. Konigsburg, E. L.
Westmark. Alexander, Lloyd.

Level 6

Alan and Naomi. Levoy, Myron.
(The) Alfred Summer. Slepian, Jan.
Bingo Brown, Gypsy Lover. Byars, Betsy.
Blackberries in the Dark. Jukes, Mavis.
Borrowed Children. Lyon, George Ella.
Cousins. Hamilton, Virginia.
A Day No Pigs Would Die. Peck, Robert Newton.
(The) Empty Sleeve. Garfield, Leon.
Finding David Dolores. Willey, Margaret.
A Fine White Dust. Rylant, Cynthia.
(The) Ghost Belonged to Me. Peck, Richard.
Hatchet. Paulson, Gary.
(The) Keeper. Naylor, Phyllis.
(The) Machine Gunners. Westall, Robert.
(The) Man from the Other Side. Orlev, Uri.
My Brother Sam Is Dead. Collier, James Lincoln.

One-Eyed Cat. Fox, Paula.
On the Edge. Cross, Gillian.
Phantom Tollbooth. Juster, Norton.
Prairie Songs. Conrad, Pam.
Risk'n Roses. Slepian, Jan.
(The) Shimmershine Queens. Yarbrough, Camille.
A String in the Harp. Bond, Nancy.
Summer of the Swans. Byars, Betsy.
Sweetgrass. Hudson, Jan.
Taking Sides. Soto, Gary.
True Confessions of Charlotte Doyle. Avi.
Where the Wild Lilies Bloom. Cleaver, Vera and Cleaver, Bill.
Words by Heart. Sebestyen, Ovida.
Young Landlords. Myers, Walter Dean.

DLM
PO Box 4000, One DLM Park, Allen, TX 75002
1-800-527-4747
Bill Martin's Sounds of Language Books. Grades 1–4.
Bill Martin's Treasure Chest of Poetry. Pre K–3.

Harcourt Brace Jovanovich/Holt Rinehart and Winston
School Department, National Customer Service Center, Dowden Road
Orlando, FL 32887
1-800-225-5425

LINK, The Language Company
1675 Carr Street, Suite 209-N, Lakewood, CO 80215
1-800-637-7993
LINK-PAKS, activities for extended lessons. Pre K–7.

Modern Curriculum Press
13900 Prospect Road, Cleveland, OH 44136
1-800-321-3106
Big Books and Language Works. Grades 1–4.

Recorded Books, Inc.
270 Skipjack Road, Prince Frederick, MD 20678
1-800-638-1304
Audio Recordings of Books. Elementary–High School.

Rigby
PO Box 797, Crystal Lake, IL 60014
1-800-822-8661
Informational Collections. K–6; *Storybook Collections.* Pre K–4.

Scholastic Canada
123 Newkirk Road, Richmond Hill, Ontario L4C3G5
Reflexions (1991–1994) Books for Whole Language Programs. K–8.

Scholastic U.S.
PO Box 7502, Jefferson City, MO 65102
1-800-325-6149
*Basal-Correlated Collections of Trade Books; Traditional Teaching Suggestions;
 Theme-Based Books; Books for Pleasure Reading.* K–6.

Troll
100 Corporate Drive, Mahwak, NJ 07430.
1-800-526-5289
Collections and Books for Theme-Based Units. K–6.

The Wright Group
19201 120th Avenue, Bothell, WA 98011
1-800-523-2371
Numerous Collections; Informational and Narrative Sets. K–5 (Mostly K–3).

**TABLE 5–6
Literature Programs
(Collections)**

Atheneum Publishers
597 Fifth Ave.
New York, NY 50017

Bradbury Press Inc.
(See E.P. Dutton Inc.)

Coward, McCann &
    Geoghan Inc.
(See Putnam Publishing Group)

Crowell/Lippincott Junior Books
(See Harper & Row Publishers)

Delacorte Press
One Dag Hammarskjold Press
New York, NY 10017

The Dial Press
(See Delacorte Press)

Doubleday & Company Inc.
245 Park Ave.
New York, NY 10167

E. P. Dutton Inc.
2 Park Ave.
New York, NY 10016

Farrar, Straus & Giroux Inc.
19 Union Square W.
New York, NY 10003

Four Winds
50 W. 44 Street
New York, NY 10036

Greenwillow Books
(See Morrow Junior Books)

Harcourt Brace Jovanovich Inc.
757 Third Ave.
New York, NY 10017

Harper & Row Publishers Inc.
10 E. 53 Street
New York, NY 10022

Holiday House
18 E. 53 Street
New York, NY 10022

Houghton Mifflin Company
One Beacon Street
Boston, MA 02107

Alfred A. Knopf Inc.
(See Random House Inc.)

Little, Brown & Company
34 Beacon Street
Boston, MA 02106

Lothrop, Lee & Shephard Books
(See Morrow Junior Books)

McGraw-Hill Inc.
1221 Avenue of the Americas
New York, NY 10020

Macmillan Inc.
866 3rd Ave.
New York, NY 10022

Morrow Junior Books
105 Madison Ave.
New York, NY 10016

Pantheon Books Inc.
(See Random House Inc.)

Philomel Books
(See Putnam Publishing Group)

Putnam Publishing Group
200 Madison Ave.
New York, NY 10016

Random House Inc.
201 E. 50 Street
New York, NY 10022

Simon and Schuster
One Lake Street
Upper Saddle River, NJ 07458

TABLE 5–7
Publisher Addresses

Levels 3–5

The American Family Farm. Anderson, Joan.
The Big Beast Book: Dinosaurs and How They Got That Way. Booth, Jerry.
Bill Peet: An Autobiography. Peet, Bill.
Bird Watch. Yolen, Jane.
The Book of Eagles. Sattler, Helen Roney.
Buffalo Hunt. Freedman, Russell.
Cats Are Cats. Larrick, Nancy.
China Homecoming. Fritz, Jean.
Christopher Columbus: Voyager to the Unknown. Levinson, Nancy Smiler.
Daniel Boone. Lawlor, Laurie.
*Dawn to Dusk in the Galapagos: Flightless Birds, Swimming Lizards and
    Other Fascinating Creatures.* Gelman, Rita Golden.
Dinosaur Dig. Lasky, Kathryn.
Eye Witness Books
Good Queen Bess: The Story of Elizabeth I of England. Stanley, Diane and
    Vennema, Peter.
Growing Up Amish. Ammon, Richard.
Indian Chiefs. Freedman, Russell.
Lincoln: A Photobiography. Freedman, Russell.
Living with Dinosaurs. Lauber, Patricia.
Neptune. Simon, Seymour.
Ramona: Behind the Scenes of a Television Show. Scott, Elaine.
Skeleton. Parker, Steve.
The Story of Football. Anderson, Dave.
Tales Mummies Tell. Lauber, Patricia.

Level 6 and Above

Children of the Maya: A Guatemalan Indian Odyssey. Ashbranner, Brent.
Circus Dreams: The Making of a Circus Artist. Cushman, Kathleen and
    Miller, Montana.
Columbus and the World Around Him. Meltzer, Milton.
Franklin Delano Roosevelt. Freedman, Russell.
Now Is Your Time! The African American Struggle for Freedom. Myers,
    Walter Dean.
Prairie Visions: The Life and Time of Salomon Butcher. Conrad, Pam.
Seeing Earth from Space. Lauber, Patricia.
Vietnam: Why We Fought. Hoobler, Dorothy and Hoobler, Thomas.
Woodsong. Paulsen, Gary.

TABLE 5–8
Nonfiction Books   *The Wright Brothers: How They Invented the Airplane.* Freedman, Russell.

TABLE 5–9 "Summer Reading" Book Lists

Level K–3

Award-Winning Collection

Adventures of Ali Baba Bernstein. (IRA Children's Choice)
Alexander and the Wind-Up Mouse. (Caldecott Honor Book)
Ben's Trumpet. (Caldecott Honor Book)
Chair for My Mother. (Caldecott Honor Book)
Each Peach Pear Plum. (Kate Greenaway Medal)
Farmer in the Soup. (IRA Children's Choice)
Frog and Toad Together. (Newbery Honor Book)
Freight Train. (Caldecott Honor Book)
Haunting of Grade Three. (IRA Children's Choice)
Hundred Dresses. (Newbery Honor Book)
Hundred Penny Box. (Newbery Honor Book)
In the Forest. (Caldecott Honor Book)
Little Island. (Caldecott Honor Book)
Madeline. (Caldecott Honor Book)
Mufaro's Beautiful Daughters. (Caldecott Honor Book)

Nettie's Trip South. (IRA Children's Choice)
On Market Street. (Caldecott Honor Book)
Owl Moon. (Caldecott Honor Book)
Pecos Bill. (SLJ Best Book)
Pigs in Hiding. (SLJ Best Book)
Rose in My Garden. (SLJ Best Book)
Snowy Day. (Caldecott Medal)
Song and Dance Man. (Caldecott Medal)
Stone Soup. (IRA Children's Choice)
Stringbean's Trip to the Shining Sea. (SLJ Best Book)
Swimmy. (Caldecott Honor Book)
Ten, Nine, Eight. (Caldecott Honor Book)
Visit to Washington, DC. (IRA Children's Choice)
White Snow, Bright Snow. (Caldecott Medal)
Why Mosquitoes Buzz in People's Ears. (Caldecott Medal)

Hobbies, Activities, and Humor

Addition Wipe-Off Book
All About the Weather
Animals at Home Sticker Book
Bunny Bakeshop
Clifford's Riddles
Ed Emberley's Drawing Book of Animals
Fabulous Greeting Cards to Make
How to Draw Cartoons
How to Draw Horses
How to Draw Silly Monsters
I Can Draw Cartoon Characters
I Can Draw Planes and Helicopters
I Can Draw Prehistoric Animals

Is It Red? Is It Yellow? Is It Blue?
It Zwibble Springtime Activity Book
Letters and Sounds
Lucky Book of Riddles
Magic Mirror
Magic Science Tricks
My Birthday Book
No Cook Cookbook
101 Wacky Science Jokes
Simple Science Says: Take One Compass
Simple Science Says: Take One Mirror
26 Letters and 99 Cents

Social Studies

Angel Child, Dragon Child
Baby Sister for Frances
Big City Port
Chair for My Mother
Christopher Columbus
Curious George at the Airport
Curious George Takes a Job
I Am Eyes Ni Macho
Ira Says Goodbye
Ira Sleeps Over
Johnny Appleseed
Legend of the Blue Bonnet
Little Island

Martin Luther King Day
MudPony
Nettie's Trip South
New Coat for Anna
Oh, What a Thanksgiving
Pilgrim's First Thanksgiving
Round Trip
Trains
True Stories about Abraham Lincoln
Visit to Washington, DC
What Mary Jo Shared
Where the Forest Meets the Sea

Values and Self Esteem

Alexander and the Wind-Up Mouse
Angel Child, Dragon Child
Baby Sister for Frances

Bargain for Frances
Bedtime for Frances
Birthday for Frances

(Cont.)

TABLE 5–9   *(Cont.)*

Values and Self Esteem

Bread and Jam for Frances
Chair for My Mother
Crow Boy
Elves and the Shoemaker
Emperor's New Clothes
Franklin in the Dark
Jamaica's Find
King Midas and the Golden Touch
Little Rabbit's Baby Brother
Little Red Hen

Lucky's Choice
Mufaro's Beautiful Daughters
Newsman Ned and the Broken Rules
Noisy Nora
Swimmy
10 for Dinner
Terrible Thing That Happened at Our House
What Mary Jo Shared
Where the Forest Meets the Sea

Science

Animal Shelters
Ant Cities
Backyard Insects
Book about Planets and Stars
Busy Beavers
Chickens Aren't the Only Ones
Day in Space
Day Underwater
Dinosaur Time
Dinosaurs and More Dinosaurs
First Dinosaurs
Koko's Story

Magic School Bus: At the Waterworks
Magic School Bus: Inside the Human Body
Pumpkin Pumpkin
Real Robots
Reason for a Flower
Seed Is a Promise
Snakes
Snow and Ice
Story of George Washington Carver
Turtle and Tortoise
Very Hungry Caterpillar
Wind

Level 4–6

Award-Winning Collection

A, My Name is Ami. (IRA Children's Choice)
Adam of the Road. (Newbery Medal)
Apple and the Arrow. (Newbery Honor Book)
Call It Courage. (Newbery Medal)
Can't You Make Them Behave, King George? (SLJ Best Book)
Cat Who Went to Heaven. (Newbery Medal)
Christina's Ghost. (IRA Children's Choice)
Circle of Gold. (Coretta Scott King Honor Book)
Cybil War. (SLJ Best Book)
Door in the Wall. (Newbery Medal)
Exploring the Titanic. (SLJ Best Book)
Fourteen and Holding. (IRA Children's Choice)
Friendship Pact. (IRA Children's Choice)
Ghosts Between Our Feet. (IRA Children's Choice)
I Want to Go Home! (IRA Children's Choice)
Invincible Louisa. (Newbery Medal)
Little House in the Big Woods. (Newbery Honor Book)

Long Winter. (Newbery Honor Book)
Miracles on Maple Hill. (Newbery Medal)
Misty of Chincoteague. (Newbery Medal)
More Tales for the Midnight Hour. (IRA Children's Choice)
My Side of the Mountain. (Newbery Honor Book)
Old Yeller. (Newbery Honor Book)
Our Man Weston. (IRA Children's Choice)
Phantom Tollbooth. (Newbery Honor Book)
Secret of NIMH. (Newbery Medal)
Tales from Silver Lands. (Newbery Medal)
These Happy Golden Years. (Newbery Honor Book)
Will You Sign Here, John Hitchcock? (IRA Children's Choice)
Wish Giver. (Newbery Honor Book)

Hobbies, Activities and Humor

Across the USA Game
Calligraphy Book
Chocolate! Chocolate! Chocolate!
Drawing Book
Easy Cooking for Kids
Fabulous Facts about the Fifty States
Freshwater Fish and Fishing
Great Meals, Great Snacks, Great Kids

How to Make a Zero Backwards
How to Write Codes and Send Secret Messages
Karate
Laugh-a-Minute Joke Book
My Writing Book
101 Bossy Cow Jokes
101 Bug Jokes
101 Elephant Jokes

(Cont.)

Social Studies

Apple and the Arrow	*How the White House Really Works*
By the Shores of Silver Lake	*Lost Star: Story of Amelia Earhart*
Custer and Crazy Horse	*Mr. President: Book of U.S. Presidents*
Death of Lincoln	*Plain Girl*
Destination: Antarctica	*Pocahantas and the Strangers*
First Woman Doctor	*Secret Missions*
Freedom Crossing	*Slave Ship*
Great Escapes from W.W.II	

Values and Self Esteem

Amanda the Cut Up	*Miracle at Clement's Pond*
Apple and the Arrow	*Mom, You're Fired!*
Between Friends	*My Side of the Mountain*
Call It Courage	*My Sister, the Meanie*
Christmas Carol	*One Step at a Time*
Darci and the Dance Contest	*Snow Treasure*
Does Anybody Care about Lou Emma Miller?	*Summer of Mrs. MacGregor*
Door in the Wall	*Too Many Murphys*
Follow My Leader	*Truth or Dare*
Good-bye, My Wishing Star	*Veronica Ganz*
Inside Out	*With You and Without You*
Kid Power	*You Shouldn't Have to Say Good-bye*
Little Gymnast	

Science

Day We Walked on the Moon	*Sevengill: The Shark and Me*
Destination: Antarctica	*Sideways Arithmetic from Wayside School*
Exploring the Titanic	*Story of Thomas Alva Edison, Inventor*
Freshwater Fish and Fishing	*Volcanoes and Earthquakes*
King Snake	*What's Down There?*
My Side of the Mountain	*What if? 50 Discoveries That Changed the World*
Nine True Dolphin Stories	*What's Beyond? Solving Mysteries in Space*
Record Setting Animals	

TABLE 5–10 Multicultural Books

And Sunday Makes Seven (Ages 5–8)	
A County Far Away (Ages 3–6)	*Eric Carle's Animals, Animals* (Ages 6–10)
The Day of Ahmed's Secret (Ages 5–8)	*The Great Wall of China* (Ages 6–9)
A Handful of Stars (Ages 12–15)	*Hershel and the Hanukkah Goblins* (Ages 5–8)
In the Beginning: Creation Stories from Around the World (Ages 11–14)	*Iktomi and the Buffalo Bull: A Plains Indian Story* (Ages 6–9)
The Last Princess (Ages 8–12)	*Knots on a Counting Rope* (Ages 4–10)
On the Pampas (Ages 5–8)	*The Legend of the Indian Paintbrush* (Ages 7–10)
Shabanu: Daughter of the Wind (Ages 11–15)	*Lon Po Po: A Red Riding Hood Story from China* (Ages 6–9)
Two Short and One Long (Ages 9–12)	*The Microscope* (Ages 6–10)
A Wave in Her Pocket (Ages 7–10)	*Mirandy and Brother Wind* (Ages 8–11)
The Children We Remember (Ages 7–12)	*Mufaro's Beautiful Daughters* (Ages 8–11)
Chita's Christmas Tree (Ages 5–8)	*Oh Brother* (Ages 6–8)
Come-a-Tide (Ages 5–7)	*Peter and the Wolf* (Ages 4–8)
Cowboy Dreams (Ages 5–7)	*Shaka: King of the Zulus* (Ages 7–10)
The Doorbell Rang (Ages 5–7)	

	Poem Books
	Sing a Song of Popcorn: Every Child's Books of Poems. Edited by Schenk de Regniers and others.
	Where the Sidewalk Ends. Silverstein, Shel.
	A Light in the Attic. Silverstein, Shel.
	Paul Revere's Ride. Longfellow, Henry Wadsworth. Illustrated by Ted Rank.
	Whiskers and Rhymes. Lobel, Arnold.

	Poems in Picture Books
TABLE 5–11 **Poem Books** **and Poems** **in Picture Books**	*Block City.* Stevenson, Robert Louis. Illustrated by Ashley Wolff.
	My Shadow. Stevenson, Robert Louis. Illustrated by Ted Rand.
	The Owl and the Pussycat. Lear, Edward. Illustrated by Jan Brett.
	17 Kings and 42 Elephants. Mahy, Margaret. Illustrated by Patricia MacCarthy.
	The Walrus and the Carpenter. Carroll, Lewis. Illustrated by Jan Breskin.

	A Frog Prince. Berenzy, Alix.
	Goldilocks and the Three Bears. Marshall, James.
	Jim and the Beanstalk. Briggs, Raymond.
	Princess Furball. Retold by Huck, Charlotte.
	Sidney Rella and the Glass Sneaker. Myers, Bernice.
TABLE 5–12 **Fractured** **Fairy Tales**	*A Telling of Tales.* Brooke, William J.
	Trail of Stones. Strauss, Gwen.
	The True Story of the Three Little Pigs. Scieszka, Jon.

REFERENCES

Alverman, Donna E., and Phelps, Stephen E. *Content Reading and Literacy.* Needham, MA: Allyn and Bacon, 1994.

Carter, Betty, and Thomas, James L. "Big Books: Purchasing and Using Enlarged Texts." *Book Links,* November, 1991.

Carter, Betty. "Big Books." *Book Links,* May, 1992.

Cox, Carole, and Zarrillo, James. *Teaching Reading with Children's Literature.* New York: Macmillan, 1993.

Lynch, Priscilla. *Using Big Books and Predictable Books.* Ontario, Canada: Scholastic, 1986.

Perry, Denise (Ed.). *American Library Association: Best of the Best for Children.* 1992.

Roatman, Regie. *Invitations: Changing as Teachers and Learners K–12.* Toronto, Canada: Irwin; Portsmouth, NH: Heinemann, 1991.

Weaver, Constance. *Reading Process and Practice.* 2nd ed. Portsmouth, NH: Heinemann, 1994.

CHAPTER 6

Assessment (Making Sense of Standardized Tests and Using Authentic Tests)

PHILOSOPHY

For most of the twentieth century standardized, multiple-choice tests have been the popular method of assessing children's progress in schools. For most school districts it has been the most economic and efficient way to see how well schools have been educating our children and youth. Even though there have been no serious detractors until recently, there have always been critics of standardized tests.

Thoughtful concerns and a call for alternative ways to assess children developed in the late 1970s and 1980s, and today many school districts are using what is termed "authentic testing" or "performance assessment." These methods differ in style and substance from standardized tests. They are viewed as alternatives to traditional, multiple-choice, standardized achievement tests, and all refer to direct examination of student performance on significant tasks that are relevant to life outside of school as well as inside.

Proponents of alternative assessment think that standardized tests do not truly measure a student's ability to perform academic tasks. They believe that sampling contrived, out-of-context tasks, or standardized tests do not give an accurate picture of how that student would do on a real-life, in-context-task, performed in the classroom. In this chapter we will discuss the types of testing done across the United States so that teachers can evaluate the testing and inform parents and students in a more comprehensive manner. We will also address the differences between standardized tests and authentic, real-life assessment tests.

LEARNING PRINCIPLES

Principle 1—*The Nature of the Learning Process.* Learning is a natural process of pursuing personally meaningful goals that is active, volitional, and internally mediated; it is a process of discovering and constructing meaning from information and experience, filtered through each individual's unique perceptions, thoughts, and feelings.

Principle 2—*Goals of the Learning Process.* The learner seeks to create meaningful and coherent representations of knowledge regardless of the quantity and quality of data available.

The questions we will discuss are:

> I. What kinds of standardized testing are given in the United States and what are their purposes?
>
> II. What is meant by authentic assessment and what are examples of these tests?
>
> III. What are the differences between these forms of testing and what purposes are there for each type?

I. What kinds of standardized testing are given in the United States and what are their purposes? (This section addresses testing only for your knowledge, not as an endorsement of standardized testing. I believe that teachers ought to be knowledgeable about any testing that their children may have to take as long as school districts continue to use them.)

A. In the United States today there are many types of standardized tests used to determine how the schools are doing in educating children. Test selection is largely determined by the reasons for testing and there are many purposes for using tests in school districts across the United States. The ones most often stated are the following:

- To provide the general public with evidence of student growth

- To judge how well schools are educating children

- To place students in special programs by tracking them

- To pass or retain students

- To plan curriculum

- To provide information for research

- To provide data for budgetary planning and tax allotment

- To evaluate teachers

Test results are then used by many people in addition to teachers such as principals, superintendents, school boards, various curriculum committees, and so on. Each group has different reasons and purposes for looking at the tests and for using the results. Some tests measure specific skills and are closer to actual tasks performed in a classroom (although in recent years this has been disputed by many educators). Other tests provide group or survey data, which cannot be used for specific diagnostic or instructional situations. Still other types are appropriate for comparing different sets of materials so that a decision can be made concerning purchase.

Teachers, superintendents, school boards, and others need to consider the following factors in order to determine whether or not to use a particular test:

- Ease of scoring and interpretation

- Measures what it purports to measure

- Is consistent at all levels

- Is easy to administer (not too long or difficult)

Before picking a particular test for a district usually a test committee or group of concerned people come together to determine what the district wants to test. This, of course, varies from one district to another across the country. And in some states the state itself has devised a test that better meets the criteria in that particular area of the country.

B.   Standardized tests consider all the following factors:

Validity.   This describes whether a test actually measures what it intends to measure and can usually be determined by teachers themselves. Most teachers know the strengths and weaknesses of students in their particular class. They need to examine the test items and procedures to determine whether the test does what it claims to do and whether the results closely resemble the academic behavior of those children tested. It needs to measure what the children have been taught and also to approximate the particular concepts in subject areas by texts being used.

Reliability.   This tells whether a test is consistent in the information that is provided. If a test is used over and over with a group of students and continues to yield the same results, it is considered reliable. Most tests given are not 100 percent reliable because of the differences in student learning and because of environmental, physical, and emotional factors that may be present. In order to increase the percentage of reliability it is important for teachers to keep the testing situation as constant as possible. If the environment, physical, and emotional factors are regulated, the results can be more confidently attributed to learning.

Reliability estimates are usually listed in the scoring or administrative manuals provided by the publishers of tests. It is crucial that teachers read through these manuals to become familiar with these methods of determining reliability and their percentages. Three common methods are used: the split-half, test/retest, and alternate form reliability estimates. These three correlations show the degree of relationship among the factors in the three methods.

The degree of relationship is usually stated as a reliability coefficient and ranges from 1.0 (or a perfect relationship) to .80, which is also considered reliable among educators.

Standard Error of Measurement. This refers to exactly how much a score must vary by increasing or decreasing before the difference is attributed to something other than chance. It is usually stated in pluses and minuses. For example, if the student scored 7 on a possible 10-item test and the standard error of measurement was 2—the child could either have a minus 2 score of 5 or a plus score of 9. In other words the range could be from 5–7. If the child took the test again and received the score of 9, it could not be considered improvement because it would fall in the same range as the previous test. That is, they are within two points of each other and could be attributed to chance.

C. There are four types of tests that are most commonly used in schools today.

Survey Tests—Provide indications of general ability, but not specific strengths and weaknesses

Group Tests—Test many students at a time that results in saving time when a large population needs to be assessed

Individual Tests—One-on-one tests that can control conditions and permit examiners to use observations as well as results of the test to provide information

Diagnostic Tests—Tests that assess specific, designated abilities and provide information that helps determine instructional practices (See lists of tests used across the United States at the end of the chapter.)

Formal or standardized tests are referred to as either norm referenced or criterion-referenced. Let's take a look at each type:

Norm-Referenced. These tests compare a student or group to a group of similar students. They contain several subtests in various subject areas and have been used with large groups of children to determine the norm.

In picking a norm-referenced test or when asked to use one by the district, it's important to do the following:

• Carefully examine the test manuals for procedures and scoring interpretations.

• Consider whether your students are similar to the norm group for reliable or valid comparison.

The testing is conducted in a very formal, consistent manner throughout the school and usually consists of the following:

1. Instructions to be read to the students

2. Timed sections that require a stopwatch or a watch with a second hand

3. Consecutive sections to be done in order for various subject areas

4. Test booklets and answer sheets to be collected and scored electronically

5. Returned results that include several parts such as overall scores for the class; a section comparing the class to a norm group; and a section that notes the student's errors and scores along with an itemized list of certain items on the test and numbers of errors for that item in the classroom as a whole.

Norm-referenced tests are reported in the following types of norms: grade norms—grade equivalents; percentile norms—percentile scores or ranks; and standard score norms—standard scores.

Criterion-Referenced. A criterion-referenced test differs from a norm-referenced by simply comparing the student's performance to an established criterion. The student's score is compared to a predetermined criterion of success or mastery.

This type of test is generally used when teachers want to determine whether a child is ready to move on to another level of instruction. But because of the strict adherence to certain criteria at each step to determine mastery, it has been criticized. Many educators contend that it implies that all necessary subskills have been correctly sequenced and identified and that the sequence is indicative of the way in which all children learn. Although we can identify certain necessary subskills needed to master a concept, the sequence is harder to determine. Skills are often interrelated and difficult to separate.

In determining whether to use norm-referenced or criterion-referenced testing you need to consider the following:

• Both compare students to set or externally imposed criterion.

• The difference between using one or the other is minimal.

• They differ only in philosophy and the way the scores are used.

• Criterion-referenced tests are more closely keyed to an instructional use (and therefore used more often).

• Norm-referenced are generally given only once or twice a year.

D. Scoring and interpretation of the results of standardized formal testing is reported in the following ways. It is necessary for teachers to become familiar with these ways of scoring tests and the meaning of the scores so that they can accurately report the findings to parents and others.

Raw Scores. If a student responds correctly to thirty-five items on an objective test in which each item counts 1 point, the raw score is 35. Thus a raw score is simply the number of points received on a test. It doesn't make any difference if an item is weighted in any particular way. A raw score remains the number of points received.

A raw score is only meaningful when converting it into a profile indicating what tasks it suggests a student can perform on either a criterion-referenced or norm-referenced test.

Percentage Scores. Percentages are calculated by dividing the number of correct responses by the total possible and then multiplying the result by 100. A raw score of 20 on both a 25-item and a 40-item test would produce percentage scores of 80 and 50 respectively.

Percentile Scores. These scores tell the percent of the norm population scoring below the pupil's score, thereby telling how the student stands within the norm group. In the example above, under percentage scores of 80 and 50 (20/25 and 20/40) would mean 80 percent of the norm group scored below the student on the 20/25 item test and 50 percent scored below the student on the 20/40 item test. Unlike percentage scores, which mask an individual's rank within a peer group, percentile scores provide information about relative standing.

Stanine Scores. These scores also give a picture of the relative standing of a pupil. Stanines indicate how students performed using a 9-point scale, in which 9 is high, 1 is low, and 5 is average. This is an easy system for reporting and is widely used for that reason. The main limitation of stanine scores is that they can't be used to show growth from one year to the next. They are criticized on the basis of being only divided into nine parts too. However, one could argue that there is a benefit of not over interpreting results. Stanines provide satisfactory discriminations in test performance for most educational uses.

Grade equivalents are used by some test companies to provide information about relative standing as well. However, in the more recent years they have been soundly criticized because of the misuse or misinterpretation of the scores. If a student receives a score of 7.0 then the student's raw score is equivalent to the average score of a beginning seventh grader in the norm population. It sounds simple but is misleading when considering the following possible misinterpretations based upon inappropriate assumptions.

Possible Misinterpretations.

1. Confusion of norms with standards of what should be. In any group 50 percent of the pupils in the standardized group are above the norm and 50 percent are below. So, we should not interpret a particular grade norm as something all students should attain. If we are teaching pupils who have above average ability, merely matching the norm would be a concern. If, however, we are teaching students of lower ability, reaching the norm may be considered good.

2. Placing students in a grade according to grade equivalent scores. Some teachers have misused grade equivalent scores by using them to place students. For example, we might conclude that a fifth-grade student should be doing sixth-grade work if she earns a grade equivalent of 6.0 on a test. This assumption overlooks the fact that she can obtain a score well above her grade level by doing less difficult test items more

rapidly and accurately than her fifth-grade classmates. It may simply mean she has mastered the skills taught in the first five grades. Thus grade equivalents are based on the average performance of pupils at various grade levels. As we have seen, however, they have limitations that can lead to misinterpretation and are not useful for reporting growth or level. In fact, the International Reading Association is opposed to the grade equivalent score entirely and, consequently, have caused many test publishers to discontinue reporting them.

II. What is meant by authentic assessment and what are examples of these tests?

    A. According to Grant Wiggins (1992), who has been instrumental in promoting authentic testing, the eight basic design criteria that follow should be considered:[1]

        1. Assessment tasks should be, whenever possible, authentic and meaningful—worth mastering.

        2. The set of tasks should be a valid sample from which apt generalizations about overall performance of complex capacities can be made.

        3. The scoring criteria should be authentic, with points awarded or taken off for essential successes and errors, not for what is easy to count or observe.

        4. The performance standards that anchor the scoring should be genuine benchmarks, not arbitrary cut scores or provincial school norms.

        5. The context of the problems should be rich, realistic, and enticing—with the inevitable constraints on access to time, resources, and advance knowledge of the tasks and standards appropriately minimized.

        6. The tasks should be validated.

        7. The scoring should be feasible and reliable.

        8. Assessment results should be reported and used so that all customers for the data are satisfied.

    B. The NAEYC (National Association for the Education of Young Children) 1991 position statement lists the following guidelines for appropriate assessment:[2]

        1. Curriculum and assessment are integrated throughout the program; assessment is congruent with and relevant to the goals, objectives, and content of the program.

        2. Assessment results in benefits to the child or children and improvements in the program.

        3. Children's development and learning in all the domains—physical, social, emotional, and cognitive—and their dispositions and feelings are informally and routinely assessed by teachers.

4. Informal and routine assessment consists of teachers' observing children's performance and interactions, listening to them as they talk, and using children's constructive errors to understand their learning.

5. Assessment involves regular and periodic observation of the child in a wide variety of circumstances that are representative of the child's behavior in the program over time.

6. Assessment relies primarily on procedures that reflect the ongoing life of the classroom and typical activities of the children. Assessment avoids approaches that place children in artificial situations, impede the usual learning and developmental experiences in the classroom, or divert children from their natural learning processes.

7. Assessment relies on demonstrated performance, during real, not contrived activities, for example, real reading and writing activities rather than only skills testing (Engel, 1990; Teale, 1988).

8. Assessment utilizes an array of tools and a variety of processes including but not limited to collections or representative work by children (art work, stories they write, tape recordings of their reading), records of systematic observations by teachers, records of conversations and interviews with children, and teachers' summaries of children's progress as individuals and as groups (Goodman, Goodman, & Hood, 1989).

9. Assessment recognizes individual diversity of learners and allows for differences in styles and rates of learning.

10. Assessment supports children's development and learning; it does not threaten children's psychological safety or feelings or self-esteem.

11. Assessment supports parents' relationships with their children and does not undermine parents' confidence in their children's or their own ability.

12. Assessment demonstrates children's overall strengths and progress, what children can do, not just their wrong answers or what they cannot do or do not know.

13. Assessment is an essential component of the teacher's role. Since teachers can make maximal use of assessment results, the teacher is the primary assessor.

14. Assessment is a collaborative process involving children and teachers, teachers and parents, school and community. Information from parents about each child's experiences at home is considered in planning instruction and evaluating children's learning. Information obtained from assessment is shared with parents.

15. Assessment encourages children to participate in self-evaluation.

16. Assessment addresses what children can do independently and what they can demonstrate with assistance, since the latter shows the direction of their growth.

17. Information about each child's growth, development, and learning is systematically collected and recorded at regular intervals. Information such as samples of children's work, descriptions of their performance, and anecdotal records is used for planning instruction and communicating with parents.

18. A regular process exists to share information with parents periodically about their child's growth and development and performance. The method of reporting to parents does not rely on letter or numerical grades, but rather provides more meaningful, descriptive information in narrative form.

C. Examples of "authentic tests" would be anything you do to assess children's performance that is meaningful, multimodal, ongoing, and occurring in authentic settings.

Authentic assessment isn't a single method. It includes performance tests, observations, or open-ended questions where students tackle a problem but there's no single right answer; exhibitions (portfolios, interviews, and so forth) in which children choose their own ways to demonstrate what they have learned.

The following activities and experiences constitute authentic assessment for a classroom.

1. Observations—keeping anecdotal records listing children's strengths, weaknesses, needs progress, learning style, skills and strategies mastered. They should be brief, consistent, and factual. They need to be collected during classroom activities on a regular basis. Teachers use post-it notes, clipboard notebooks, rolodexes, and so forth for collection.

2. Surveys/Interviews—It's easy to begin the year by taking a survey of your students interests, attitudes toward certain subject areas, and so on. Another approach is through interviews with individual children. These should be ongoing and done on a weekly basis. I usually scheduled them during self-selected reading time, journal writing time, or another special time when you can squeeze in 3–5 minutes per child.

3. Checklists—I usually constructed checklists to note mastery of a particular strategy or skill I was modeling and had children practice.

4. Retellings—This is, I think, one of the very best ways to see how your children are progressing in any area. You are simply asking them to tell or write in their own words what they learned. In reading, it can be a retelling of the story. In math, it can be an explanation of how they solved a problem. In science and social studies, it can be how much they remember about concepts, experiments, and so forth.

5. Running Records or Miscue Analysis—These are good ways to see how children are progressing in reading. They are easy

to administer and can be done quarterly or semi-annually to see how your children are progressing.

6. Teacher-Made-Tests—Teachers have always made short-question tests for children to take after reading something. Children may or may not use a book to find the answers, and it may be essay or multiple choice in construction. Sometimes with older students teachers have them develop the questions. Or another way is to have students list events or main points of what they've studied.

7. Journal Writing—Journals are a good way to evaluate progress in writing abilities, grammar usage, spelling, phonics, hand-writing, and so on. I usually collected them on a weekly basis and noted on a checklist how well they were doing.

8. Self-Evaluations—These can take many forms: checklists, reflection logs, weekly progress forms, report cards, and so forth.

9. Portfolios—These will be discussed in depth in a later chapter.

III. What are the differences between these forms of testing and what are the purposes for each type?

A Very Important Difference in Using Informal or Authentic Tests

Using a test that you construct, that is relevant to what's being taught in the classroom, is a way to make ongoing observations of a student's progress. Not only do you know from the quiz or essay test you make up, how the student performed, but you can also make observations about that child when the skill or concept is explained. This will tell you not only the end result but the process by which the child learned. This gives you valuable information to use in reteaching.

Observations should be done routinely in the following areas of development:

Cognitive—constructing numerical, spatial and temporal relation-ships; exploring, interpreting, and using problem-solving strategies.

Language—receptive and expressive, ability to communicate, listen and speak effectively, understand different forms of commun-ication.

Physical, Emotional, Social—health and fitness, gross and fine mo-tor control, self-awareness, self-control, curiosity, initiative, positive relationships with peers and adults.

A. Guidelines for Recording Observations:

1. Only record what is observed—don't try to analyze it.

2. Record some information everyday—make it part of your regu-lar routine.

3. Do two kinds of observations—focused and spontaneous. You will want to focus on a particular child at times because of problems that a child has exhibited, and so you will plan or focus on that child during a lesson or self-selected reading/ writing time. Or you may want to just watch a student because of an upcoming conference or report period. You will need to plan these focused observations so that you don't miss those quiet students who need your time and attention. Every student in your room should be observed at least once a week. Next, you should always watch for a spontaneous incident that may help you to understand or get to know a child better, academically or socially. You can provide more individually appropriate lessons if you truly know your students.

4. Plan a way to record your observations. It can be done on index cards, a spiral or regular notebook, sticky notes on a seating chart, a clipboard, or any other method that is comfortable to you. It may take a period of trial and error before you find a suitable way, but don't give up because it is worth the time and effort.

B. Tests are generally considered to be either formal or informal and fall into these three categories.

1. Teacher-Made—These tests usually take the form of short quizzes or essay questions teachers use to determine learning after lessons or units of work directly taught. There is no standardization of the results. The teacher herself determines scoring criteria, administration, and use of results. Teacher-made tests are used for:

a. Evaluating mastery of content in any subject area in order to plan further lessons.

b. Assisting in reporting progress to parents, administrators, or students themselves.

c. Determining possible groups for additional practice on skills, strategies, or concepts.

2. Informal Tests—These tests are often published by others such as tests accompanying basal readers or texts used, but the teacher's judgment in administering, scoring, and interpretation is important in determining the results. Because of her personal knowledge and familiarity with her students, she is more apt to know when to use the tests, how they should be used, and whether they are reliable. It is important, however, that the teacher follow the general procedures given in the directions. Informal tests or authentic assessments are used for:

a. Evaluating learning outcomes and content that are actually taking place in classrooms.

b. Evaluating day-to-day progress of students.

c. Evaluating knowledge of the ever-changing concepts and development in subject areas such as science and social studies.

3. Formal Tests—These tests are purchased by the district from publishers and are referred to as standardized tests. They have very specific guidelines for administration, scoring, and interpretation. Formal or standardized tests are most often used for:

a. Evaluating student's progress in basic skills and in the learning of objectives/outcomes in certain subject areas.

b. Evaluation of pupil progress.

c. Grouping pupils for instruction.

d. Determining strengths and weaknesses of students in subjects.

e. Comparison of general level of achievement with ability of students.

ENDNOTES

1. Grant Wiggins, *Creating Tests Worth Taking* (Educational Leadership, May, 1992) pp. 26–33.

2. NAEYC. *Position Statement,* Guidelines for Appropriate Assessment, March, 1991.

REFERENCES

Anthony, Robert J.; Johnson, Terry D.; Mickelson, Norma I.; Preece, Alison. *Evaluating Literacy;* (1991) Portsmouth, NH. Heinemann.

Brown, Hazel; Cambourne, Brian; *Read and Retell.* (1987) Portsmouth, NH. Heinemann.

Goodman, K. S.; Goodman, Y. M. and Hood, W. S. (Eds.), The Whole Language Evaluation Book. Portsmouth, NH. Heinemann, 1989.

Leu, Donald J.; and Kinzer; Charles K. Effective Reading Instructions K–12. 2nd ed. New York: Macmillan, 1991, pp. 433–488.

Reider, R. B.; Kinzer, C. K. *Test Preferences and Competencies of Field Educators.* In J. Niles and L. Harris, (Eds.), New Inquiries in Reading Research and Instruction, Rochester, N.Y. National Reading Conference, 1982.

Routman, Regie. Invitations: Changing as Teachers and Learners K–12. Toronto, Canada: Irwin; Portsmouth, NH: Heinemann, 1991.

Wiggins, Grant. *Teaching to the Authentic Test.* Educational Leadership, pp. 41–47, April, 1986.

Worthen, Blaine R. *Critical Issues that will Determine the Future of Alternative Assessment.* Phi Delta Kappan, February, 1993.

JOURNALS ON TESTING/MEASUREMENT

American Educational Research Journal

Applied Measurement in Education

Applied Psychological Measurement

Educational Measurement: Issues and Practice

Journal of Educational Measurement

Journal of Educational Psychology

Journal of Special Education

Review of Educational Research

TEST PUBLISHERS

1. American Guidance Service Inc.
   Publishers Building
   Circle Pines, Minnesota 55014

2. C.P.S. Inc.
   P.O. Box 83
   Larchmont, New York 10538

3. CTB/McGraw-Hill
   Del Monte Research Park
   Monterey, California 93940

4. Educational Testing Service
   Princeton, New Jersey 08540

5. Psychological Assessment Resources
   P.O. Box 998
   Odessa, Florida 33556

6. Psychological Corporation
   555 Academic Court
   San Antonio, Texas 78204

ACHIEVEMENT TESTS

Bader Reading and Language Inventory

Basic Achievement Skills Individual Screener

Brigance Diagnostic Comprehensive Inventory of Basic Skills. Braille Edition. Vols. 1–5. Green Level

California Achievement Tests. Fifth Edition (CAT/5)

California Achievement Tests. Forms E and F

Comprehensive Testing Program III. Levels A–F

Comprehensive Tests of Basic Skills. Form U and V

Comprehensive Tests of Basic Skills. Fourth Edition Levels K–14. Benchmark Tests

Comprehensive Tests of Basic Skills. Fourth Edition Levels K–14. Complete Battery

Comprehensive Tests of Basic Skills. Fourth Edition Level K. Survey Tests

Comprehensive Tests of Basic Skills. Fourth Edition Level 10. Survey Tests

Comprehensive Tests of Basic Skills. Fourth Edition Level 11. Survey Tests

Comprehensive Tests of Basic Skills. Fourth Edition Level 12. Survey Tests

Comprehensive Tests of Basic Skills. Fourth Edition Level 13. Survey Tests

Comprehensive Tests of Basic Skills. Fourth Edition Level 14. Survey Tests

Country School Examinations

Curriculum Frameworks Assessment Supplement, Level 1

Curriculum Frameworks Assessment Supplement, Level 2

Curriculum Frameworks Assessment Supplement, Level 3

Curriculum Frameworks Assessment System, Level 1

Curriculum Frameworks Assessment System, Level 2

Curriculum Frameworks Assessment System, Level 3

DST: Achievement, Science, Social Studies, Literature and the Arts

Diagnostic Achievement Battery, Second Edition

Educational Development Series, Revised, Level 13A

Iowa Tests of Basic Skills, Forms G and H, Level 5

Iowa Tests of Basic Skills, Forms G and H, Level 6

Iowa Tests of Basic Skills, Forms G and H, Level 7

Iowa Tests of Basic Skills, Forms G and H, Level 8

Iowa Tests of Basic Skills, Forms G and H, Level 9

Iowa Tests of Basic Skills, Form G, Multilevel Battery, Levels 9–14, Basic Battery

Iowa Tests of Basic Skills, Forms G and H, Multilevel Battery, Levels 9-14, Complete Battery

Iowa Tests of Basic Skills, Form J, Multilevel Battery, Levels 9–14

Iowa Tests of Basic Skills, Form J, Level 5, Early Primary Battery

Iowa Tests of Basic Skills, Primary Battery, Form J, Level 7

Iowa Tests of Basic Skills, Primary Battery, Form J, Level 8

Kaufman Assessment Battery for Children

Kaufman Test of Educational Achievement, Brief Form

Kaufman Test of Educational Achievement, Comprehensive Form

Martinez Assessment of the Basic Skills: Criterion-Referenced Diagnostic Testing of Basic Skills

Metropolitan Achievement Tests, Seventh Edition, Forms S and T

Metropolitan Achievement Tests, Sixth Edition, Survey Battery

Monitoring Basic Skills Progress, Basic Math

Monitoring Basic Skills Progress, Basic Reading

Monitoring Basic Skills Progress, Basic Spelling

National Achievement Test, Level A

National Achievement Test, Level B

National Achievement Test, Level C

National Achievement Test, Level D

National Achievement Test, Level E

Peobody Individual Achievement Test, Revised

SRA Survey of Basic Skills

Screening Children for Related Early Educational Needs

Stanford Achievement Test, Seventh Edition

Stanford Early School Achievement Test, Third Edition, Level 1 and Level 2

WICAT Test of Basic Skills

Wide Range Achievement Test, Revised

Woodcock-Johnson Psycho-Educational Battery, Revised. Tests of Achievement, Standard Battery and Supplement Battery

Individual Achievement Tests Grades

Basic Achievement Skills Individual	1–A
Screens (9)	
Peobody Ind. Ach. Test R (1)	K–A
Woodcock Reading Mastery Test R (1)	K–12

Diagnostic Tests

Grades

California Diagnostic Reading Tests (3)	1–12
Metropolitan Achievement Tests	
Language Diagnostic tests (9)	1–9.9
Reading Diagnostic Tests (9)	K.5–9.9
Stanford Diagnostic Reading Test (9)	1.5–12

Reading Tests

Grades

Gates-McGinitie Reading Tests (10)	K–12
Iowa Silent Reading Tests (9)	6–14
Nelson Reading Skills Test (10)	3–9
Nelson-Denny Reading Test (10)	9–16A

Grades

Learning Ability Tests

Cognitive Abilities Test (10)	K–12
Culture-Fair Intelligence Test (6)	4–16, A
Educational Ability Series (12)	K–12
Otis-Lennon School Ability Tests (9)	1–12
Tests of Cognitive Skills (3)	2–12

Grades

Readiness Tests

Boehm Tests of Basic Concepts (9)	K–2
Metropolitan Readiness Test (9)	K–1
Tests of Basic Experience (3)	P–1

Grades

Interest Inventory

Kuder General Interest Survey (12)	6–12

Grades

IRI's Informal Reading Inventories

Silveroli Classroom Reading Inventory	1–9
Johns, J. L. Classroom Reading Inventory	1–9

OTHER INFORMAL TESTS TO TRY

1. Read and Retell from book entitled *Read and Retell* by Brown and Cambourne, Heinemann Publishers, Portsmouth, N.H. (1987)

2. Miscue Analysis from article "Analysis of Reading Miscues" in *Reading Research Quarterly,* 5.1, 1969 and other subsequent articles by Kenneth S. Goodman. Also read his latest book entitled *Phonics Phacts,* Heinemann Publishers, Portsmouth, N.H. (1993)

3. Running Record from book entitled *The Early Detection of Reading Difficulties* by Marie M. Clay, Heinemann Publishers, Portsmouth, N.H. (1990). See this book and later editions for more tests and ideas.

4. Constructing Your Own Informal Reading Inventory or I.R.I. in book entitled *Effective Reading Instruction K–8,* 2nd ed. by Donald J. Leu and Charles K. Kinzer. MacMillan Publishers, N.Y. (1991)

CHAPTER 7

Designing Rubrics and Setting Criteria

PHILOSOPHY

Independent learning, which emanates from modeling and practice, needs to be evaluated by the students themselves. We can never measure a child's success by letter grades or arbitrary marking systems. Grading is not evaluation. It is a letter or number system that gives us little information about a child's progress. Nonetheless, grading is something most teachers have to use. School districts still have report cards that need to be addressed. The way in which I suggest using report cards is to consider what a child is accomplishing in relationship to himself and for analyzing and comparing growth. In this chapter we will discuss how to design scoring rubrics and set criteria for evaluating your students. Remembering that you are modeling first and then asking your students to continue on their own.

LEARNING PRINCIPLES

Principle 1—*The Nature of the Learning Process.* Learning is a natural process of pursuing personally meaningful goals that is active, volitional, and internally mediated; it is a process of discovering and constructing meaning from information and experience, filtered through each individual's unique perceptions, thoughts, and feelings.

Principle 3—*The Construction of Knowledge.* The learner organizes information in ways that associate and link new information with existing knowledge in uniquely meaningful ways.

The questions we will address are:

> I. What is a rubric? What are examples of these scoring forms?
>
> II. How do I teach my students to design their own criteria for a project?
>
> III. How do I use criteria across the curriculum so that I am sure learning is taking place?

I. What is a rubric? What are examples of these scoring forms? In it's most simple form a rubric is a way to record what a child has accomplished on a given task. The form it takes only has meaning when the criteria for performing the task is clearly understood.

   A. Let us begin by considering how we would make rubrics to record a child's progress in reading/writing. But, before constructing any rubrics, it is important to develop your philosophy of literacy. Any rubrics you construct or develop need to conform to your beliefs about the area of reading/writing instruction. Consider the following "Recommendations from the National Council of Teachers of English" (1988): "Teachers should develop, individually or with others, a clear position of their own on how reading/writing is best taught.[1]

   • They should continually examine this position as they work with children.

   • They should examine policies and instructional materials from this professional perspective.

   • They should keep themselves well-informed about developments in research and practice.

   • They should communicate to administrators their own professional views.

   Teachers individually and collectively need to take back the authority and responsibility to their classrooms for making basic decisions. There are many opportunities, as I have mentioned in other chapters, for you to allow and foster independence without relinquishing your authority and responsibility. You make the basic decisions and with those parameters allow and foster independence according to the level and type of class you are teaching.

   • They need to make their own decisions about how they use materials including, or not including, basals to meet the needs of their pupils.

   • They need to be willing to take risks while asserting their professional judgments.

   B. There are three models of teaching reading to which most teachers subscribe. They are as follows:

      1. A Skill-Based Reading/Writing System

         (a) Teach lessons from the teacher's manual provided by a basal reading series (or anthology).

         (b) Complete instructional activities in workbooks, dittoes, and so forth. (those listed in teacher's guide).

         (c) Additional lessons for practice are taken from the teacher's guide.

      2. A Skill-Based and Authentic Reading/Writing-Based System

         (a) All the above mentioned items.

(b) Extended lessons, for many or all stories, individually based according to students' preferences or needs.

(c) Many additional reading/writing activities that are more functional in nature (stories, original works, presentations, student designed projects, and so on).

(d) More opportunities for and emphasis on student choice.

(e) Lessons may be theme-based and integrated into all subject areas.

3. Individualized Authentic Reading/Writing-Based System

(a) Teacher models strategies students need to learn.

(b) Teacher/Students select trade books to read.

(c) Students read books alone or with partner.

(d) Student shares book with class or teacher in conference time (read and retell or some other strategy is used).

(e) Student decides on extended lesson to do alone with partner or with group that has also read the book.

(f) A portfolio system is used to keep track of work accomplished (or in progress).

(g) Lessons are more theme-based and integrated into all subject areas.

C. The decision about whether to use a published reading program is closely associated with beliefs about reading.

1. Skill-Based
Teachers who believe children learn best by following the Skill-Based philosophy stress the learning of skills first. They subscribe to the theory that children need to learn basic phonics and structural analysis skills through direct teaching of them in isolation and by practice of them in controlled, teacher-directed activities. They believe that this should be done before engaging in a lot of reading/writing on their own.

2. Skill-Based Authentic Reading/Writing
Those who subscribe to the combination Skill-Based and Authentic Reading/Writing System believe that children need to learn the skills through direct teaching, but also should be practicing those skills as they do authentic reading/writing activities in the classroom. They also think children should be able to express their own individuality by being allowed some choices in what they read and write.

3. Individualized Authentic Reading/Writing
Teachers who favor Individualized Authentic Reading/Writing believe that children should learn skills naturally (as they learned to walk and talk) by being provided with many opportunities to read and write in their own way and according to their own individual schemata. These teachers believe that in

their own learning process they acquire the basic skills of phonics and language structure and practice them each day (if allowed to do so) through choice in their reading/writing tasks. (Because of the empowerment now being given teachers, some are forming their own views of teaching the language arts and may be changing from one or another of the systems described.)

Whatever instruction appeals to you and is the one you will use, has a lot to do with the rubrics you will construct with your children. Of course, the Individualized Authentic Reading/Writing method will require devising the most rubrics, as you will not have any provided by a reading publishing company.

D. Let us consider what you might construct for a child who is already completing exercises in a workbook or dittos or both.

Your first steps might be to consider what additional knowledge you need to obtain that will help you to know your individual children's strengths and weaknesses in reading/writing, and to determine what you consider to be most important in the skills and concepts emphasized by the book company.

You will need to closely examine the teacher's guide for the list of stories you will present and ask these questions.

1. Do the stories selected provide the children with a complete understanding of the meanings and concepts they are intending to convey? (You will need to read them carefully.)

2. What additional books or stories would enrich the meanings and concepts? Make a list for each unit.

3. What skills/concepts are taught in the stories? Do you think they are of equal importance? Which ones do you think are most important for your individual class? (Remember you know your class best.) Do the following:

   (a) Study the scope and sequence for your grade level (found in the teacher's guide).

   (b) Decide which skills you consider important for your students to learn.

   (c) Directly teach those skills through content.

   (d) Set up ongoing evaluations using rubrics that you've devised.

   (e) Arrange for small groups to practice any skills not learned.

4. What activities could you use to help your children that are not listed in the guide such as journals, writing/book fairs, literacy clubs, or other sources? (See Chapter 3 for additional ideas.)

E. Now you need to plan a way to score or evaluate your children's progress in these additional stories or activities. The following types of rubrics could be used.

1. Class concept or project (simply set a continuum denoting mastery by words checked).

   (a) Concept understood, not understood.

   (b) Projects would be evaluated by a different set of terms or numbers such as: Perseverance—Confidence—Creativity

2. Specific skills listing what the skill is and denoting mastery.

   (a) A checklist listing all the skills you will introduce to your children. After the skill you will check if mastered, noting the date as well.

F. If you are going to teach reading/writing by using trade books, you will need to pick trade books that help you to teach the strategies you want your children to master. Your rubrics would list the specific strategy and denote mastery or frequency of use.

   1. Individual strategy would suggest always uses strategy, sometimes, never.

   2. Class strategies would list strategies you want your students to learn in a checklist form and indicate mastery with a date following.

      Your grids might look like this:

FIGURE 7–1 Class Concept Grid

Name Mary Jones	Concept cause/effect	Understood	Not Understood	Date

FIGURE 7–2 Individual Concept Grid—Bob Smith

Concepts 1. Cause/ Effect 2. Compare/ Contrast	Understood	Not Understood	Date	Comments

FIGURE 7–3 Class Project Grid

Name 1. John P. 2. Sally N.	Project Mural Research	Perseverance	Confidence	Creativity	Date

FIGURE 7–4   Individual Project Grid—Mary Brown

Project 1. 2. 3.	Perseverance	Confidence	Creativity	Comments/Date

FIGURE 7–5   Individual Strategy—Name _____ **Date** _____

Uses Strategy DRTA KWL QAR	Always	Sometimes	Never

FIGURE 7–6 Class Strategies—Mastery Checklist

Name	D.R.T.A.	K.W.L.	Q.A.R.	Date

You will find more rubrics at the end of the chapter. Remember to pick ones that most reflect your philosophy of literacy and are suitable for your level and class.

II. How do I teach my students to design their own criteria for a project? After you have familiarized your class with rubrics by modeling, developing, and designing some, you need to let them try some on their own.

    A. First you should discuss the goals you expect them to attain. Then you need to let them assist you in planning individual goals in all the curricular areas. It makes it easier if you are teaching in an integrated manner using themes. Keep in mind that you are trying to help your students create a profile of achievement—a documented record of growth that will show progress and allow for effective and purposeful evaluation.

        When you begin using portfolios, you will be setting regular times for conferences. During this time, you will need to assess individual progress and assist the child in setting goals unique to their learning style and needs.

    B. You can also help the whole class to start by assessing the strengths and weaknesses of the children on a teacher-made test. After you determine what you want them to learn, you need to then devise a test to see how much they know.

The steps to self-evaluation and setting criteria are as follows:

1. Administer a comprehensive test to determine your students' strengths and weaknesses (if you do not already possess that information). It should be as authentic as possible giving you knowledge of writing and oral skills, basic math and reading levels and so forth.

2. Brainstorm with students about what concepts are important in producing projects. List them on the board/chart paper.

3. Discuss how to record achievement (by numbers; words such as always, sometimes, never, and so on). Let them choose the system.

4. Make it clear that setting criteria for each lesson is important and how they will need to do this across the curriculum.

5. Set specific conference times for each student every week. These times will follow the system suggested in previous chapters (3–5 minutes at the beginning of the year and increasing in time as the year progresses).

6. The first report card should be marked by you. The subsequent ones should be marked by the students and you. (And if you think your students are able, let them mark the last one by themselves.) This, of course depends on many variables (age, level, capability). Keep in mind that even kindergartners know when they understand something and, if they are encouraged to do so, can evaluate themselves in many things. Young children like faces to indicate understanding or not . . . smiling face, frowning face, or other expressions.

III. How do I use criteria across the curriculum so that I am sure learning is taking place?

A. At the beginning of the year when you are modeling strategies for your students, you need to also be setting standards in the areas of reading, writing, listening, and speaking that will reach across all curriculum areas. Let's consider each of these areas and set a framework from which you can devise your own standards.

1. Reading/Writing—Setting Standards For:

Reading aloud

Writing aloud

Partner reading

Partner writing

Guided reading

Guided writing

Independent reading

Independent writing

Listening skills

Speaking skills

2. Questions to Ask Yourself

(a) How much time am I going to allot for each of these tasks?

(b) Am I going to divide the time equally or do I want to spend more time on certain tasks?

(c) What goals do I need to set in each area?

(d) How can I involve my students in setting the criteria for each area? Or should I set the goals myself?

3. Let's consider each question.

(a) How much time am I going to allot for each task?

Since consistency and practice are both important in learning to be a good reader/writer, I would suggest that you plan to do each of these tasks every day. I believe that setting a consistent time for each during a literacy morning is the key to success.

(b) Am I going to divide the time equally or do I want to spend more time on certain tasks?

This is an individual decision based on your philosophy of literacy. I believe that the amount of time will vary as the year progresses. For example, I would spend more time on guided reading/writing early in the year as this is the time I'm modeling strategies. I would do direct teaching of skills and concepts I consider important to learning and becoming independent. So my schedule might look like this:

8:30–8:45   Morning exercises

8:45–10:30   Guided reading/writing (teaching small group/whole class strategies, skills and concepts)

10:30–10:50   Recess

10:50–11:10   Shared reading/writing (extended lessons from guided reading/writing time with partners)

11:10–11:55   Lunch time—Self-selected reading/writing

Afternoons   Theme development, math, social studies, science, or other subjects

Note: The reading/writing aloud would be incorporated during either guided or shared reading times.

(c) What goals do I need to set in each area?

You need to ask yourself what basic skills, strategies, and concepts your students need. Of course this will vary somewhat with each grade level but there are some fundamental ones that all your students benefit from learning.

4. My list includes learning:

   (a) Use of prior knowledge

      (1) How well does the student apply learning to previous experiences?

      (2) Does the student contribute to discussions regarding past experiences?

   (b) Prediction

      (1) Does the student accurately assess the story line or plot?

      (2) Does the child make good inferences while reading?

   (c) Questioning

      (1) Does the child understand and use open-ended questioning?

      (2) Is the child able to determine the type of questions to ask in a specified type of text?

   (d) Clarifying

      (1) Does the student ask questions when unclear about task or story/article being addressed?

      (2) Is the child persistent in achieving understanding?

   (e) Summarizing

      (1) Is the student capable of retelling the important elements in what has been read?

      (2) Can the child give the information in a succinct and timely manner?

   (f) Bridging (the so-what factor)

      (1) Is the student able to see the universality of a concept or idea in a written/oral piece?

      (2) Can the student connect the events in the piece to their own life or something they've read or heard about previously?

   (g) The writing process

      (1) Is the child familiar with each area of the process such as drafting, revising, editing (proofing), and publishing?

   (h) Text factors

      (1) What are the differences between narrative (fiction) and informational texts (nonfiction)?

(2) What are the elements of a story? (plot, events, problem, resolution)

(3) What are the patterns of organization? (beginning, middle, and end)

(4) What are the text features? (illustrations, connecting words, figurative speech)

(i) Additional strategies

(1) What is a strategy for identifying and learning words?

(2) What is a strategy for teaching phonics? (e.g., beginning and ending consonants, vowel patterns, digraphs, consonant clusters)

(3) What are some fix-up strategies for monitoring and regulating comprehension?

(j) Listening

(1) Is the student able to defer judgment when listening to others?

(2) Can the student pay attention mostly to content and ignore grammar or speaking skills?

(3) Can the student listen completely first before planning a response?

(4) Can the student separate facts from principles or opinion?

(k) Speaking skills

(1) Is the student able to express an opinion clearly and confidently?

(2) Can the student engage an audience by speaking loudly and effectively?

(3) Has the student learned the techniques necessary to keep the audience interested?

(4) Can the student judge the audience and vary the presentation accordingly?

Remember that communication skills are the overriding skills that are necessary for all areas of the curriculum. If students can communicate effectively both in a written and oral manner, they will do well in all subjects. It is important in school and in life to be a good communicator. So you must take the time necessary to develop these important skills.

B. How can I involve my students in setting the criteria for each area? Or should I set the criteria myself?

You need to follow the same procedure you have established for all the learning in your classroom. Make a list of goals in each area of communication using the questions I've suggested, along with your own, and plan lessons to teach them. Then when you've directly modeled and taught, allow the children to continue on their own with practice of their individual needs by providing lots of time for presentations and activities. They will develop a set of criteria of their own after sufficient opportunities to do so. Brainstorm with them and develop some criteria if necessary.

Individual Writing Log

Student	Type of Writing	Date of Peer/Teacher Conference

Individual Book Log

Student	Book Read	Discussed	Date

Essay Questions Rubric

Concepts:	Yes	Partly	No
1. Understands: point of view theme/thesis			
2. Has developed answer in orderly logical way			
3. Has organized arguments with examples/evidence to support			

Concepts:	Above	Average	Below
Draws conclusions based on facts			
Contains enough information			
Contains evidence to support conclusions			
Uses compare/contrast or suggests why conclusion is drawn			
Demonstrates good style and clarity			

Taped-Recorded Reading

Name _____ Date _____

Text Read _____ Person Completing Form _____

Read Before Taping   ☐ Yes   ☐ No

Directions: After taping rewind, listen, and answer questions below:

	Always	Sometimes	Never
Does the reader recognize and respond to punctuation?			
Does the reader lose her or his place?			
Does the reader mispronounce words?			
Does the reader run words together?			
Does the reader self-correct?			
Does the reader realize when the meaning is not clear?			
Does the reader use fix-up strategies to clarify meaning?			
Does the reader substitute words for words in text?			
Does the reader omit words in text?			
Does the reader reverse letters/words in text?			
Does the reader read smoothly/fluently?			
Does the reader use appropriate expression?			

Comments: _____

_____

_____

Writing Survey

Name _____ Date _____

1. I think writing is _____

   _____

   _____

2. Learning about process writing has been _____

   _____

   _____

3. I like to write about _____

   _____

   _____

4. My favorite piece of writing is _____

   _____

   _____

5. Do you think you are a good writer? _____ Why? _____

   _____

   _____

Parent Survey

Dear Parent:

Please fill out the following survey. It's important for us to know about the reading/writing your child does outside school. It will also help your teacher in planning activities that are interesting/appropriate for your child. Please return to school as soon as possible.

Thank you

_____

1. Reads: ☐ Every day   2. Writes: ☐ Every day
          ☐ Almost Every day   ☐ Almost Every day
          ☐ Occasionally   ☐ Occasionally
          ☐ Never   ☐ Never

3. Reads: ☐ Stories/Books   ☐ Magazines
          ☐ Poems   ☐ Nonfiction or Informational Books
          ☐ Newspapers

4. List what child has read recently:

_____

_____

_____

5. List types of writing done (journals, letters, diary, and so on):

_____

_____

_____

6. How your child likes to read/write:

   ☐ By herself/himself

   ☐ With others

   ☐ By others

7. Comments or concerns:

_____

_____

_____

Signed _____   Date _____ / _____ / _____

Questions About Reading

Name _____ Date _____

1. I like to read about _____

_____

2. My favorite book is _____

3. My favorite author is _____

4. I like reading because _____

5. When I don't know a word I _____

6. When I don't understand I _____

7. Reading is easy when _____

8. Reading is hard when _____

Tell me what kind of reader you are _____

_____

_____

Writing Evaluation

	Yes	No

1. *Content*

    (a)   Is it focused and clear?

    (b)   Is it detailed and complete?

    (c)   Is it written from child's experiences?

2. *Organization*

    (a)   Does it have a good introduction?

    (b)   Is it written fluently and is it easy to read?

    (c)   Does it create interest?

    (d)   Does it have a climax?

    (e)   Does it have a strong conclusion?

3. *Vocabulary*

    (a)   Is the language precise?

    (b)   Are the verbs strong?

    (c)   Does it contain concrete specific nouns?

    (d)   Does the choice of words give strong imagery?

    (e)   Are the words varied and interesting?

4. *Mechanics*

    (a)   Does it contain correct spelling?

    (b)   Is the punctuation correct?

    (c)   Is the grammar correct?

    (d)   Is there attention to detail (good proofreading)?

    (e)   Is the title appropriate?

    (f)   Does it contain good margins?

Writing Evaluation

Name _____ Date _____

	Always	Sometime	Never
1. Writes during designated time.			
2. Uses good strategies.			
3. Is serious at conferences.			
4. Helps peers with drafts and revisions by listening.			
5. Accepts suggestions of peers and teacher.			
6. Offers suggestions to peers in constructive manner.			
7. Is showing growth in revising and editing work.			
8. Independently uses supports offered in room (thesauruses, dictionaries, peers, teacher).			
9. Writes for pleasure with no prompting.			
10. Willing to share writing with others.			

Teachers Comments: _____

_____

_____

Student Evaluation Form

Name _____   Group _____

Topic _____   Date _____

What did you think was the best part of your group's work? Why?

Would you change anything in this activity?

List the new things you learned from working with your group

Did you like the plan your group used? What did you especially like about it?

What additional information would you like to have on this subject?

How would you rate your group's work on a scale of 1–5?

COMMENTS: _____

_____

_____

Group Participation Evaluation

Name _____ Evaluation Date _____

	Yes	No
EXHIBITS good work habits		
TAKES PART in planning work		
PARTICIPATES in discussions		
LISTENS to opinions of others		
FOLLOWS directions given successfully		
WORKS independently		
ASSUMES leadership if asked		
RESPECTS property and materials		
HELPS in making decisions		
RETURNS material used to shelf		
FINISHES work on time		
ASSUMES responsibility for assignment		
PARTICIPATES in evaluation of work		

COMMENTS: _____

_____

_____

General Scoring Rubric

Name _____ Assignment/Skill _____

	No Understanding	Developing	Competent	Excels
Content Points 1–4				
Comments				
Process Points 1–4				
Comments				

ENDNOTES

1. National Council of Teachers of English. NCTE Urbana, Illinois, Spring Conference, 1988.

REFERENCES

Leu, Donald J., and Kinzer, Charles K. *Effective Reading Instruction, K–8,* 2nd ed. New York: Macmillan, 1991.

Brown, Jean E., Phillips, Lela B., and Stephens, Elaine C. *Toward Literacy: Theory and Applications for Teaching Writing in the Content Areas.* Belmont, California: Wadsworth, 1993.

Routman, Regie. *Invitations: Changing as Teachers and Learners K–12.* Toronto, Canada: Irwin; Portsmouth, NH: Heinemann, 1991.

CHAPTER 8

Celebrations of Learning, Portfolios, and Student-Led Conferencing

cowritten by Shelly Potter

PHILOSOPHY

After watching students perform academic tasks at every grade level for almost forty years, I really believe the best way for children to learn and retain that learning is through sharing and having choices in their presentations. All of us remember a performance in which we participated. I still remember being in a play in sixth grade! And this is why it is necessary to allow children to share their learning by some kind of celebration, portfolio projects/assignments, and student-led conferencing. When they share what they've learned (whatever it is) it is more likely to remain in their memory. We modify, revise, and use prior experiences or knowledge when we share.

LEARNING PRINCIPLES

Principle 1—*The Nature of the Learning Process.* Learning is a natural process of pursuing personally meaningful goals that is active, volitional, and internally mediated; it is a process of discovering and constructing meaning from information and experience, filtered through each individual's unique perceptions, thoughts, and feelings.

Principle 4—*Higher-Order Thinking.* Higher-order strategies for thinking about thinking—for overseeing and monitoring mental operations—facilitate creative and critical thinking and the development of expertise.

The questions we will discuss are:

I. How do we celebrate learning?

II. What are portfolios? How can they be used as meaningful and purposeful assessment tools?

III. What are student-led conferences?

IV. How can I teach my students to design their own portfolios, self-reflect, self- and peer-assess, take ownership of their work and accomplishments, and communicate with parents, peers, and others about their learning by leading their own conferences?

I. How do we celebrate learning?

According to the dictionary, to celebrate means "To praise; to make known." When we ask students to become responsible for their own learning, we must also let them show how they have done. The form that the presentation takes is not as important as what it represents. We must set high standards for the learning and never let it become a show and tell of sorts that mocks the seriousness of academic pursuits. In essence it becomes a self-evaluation of the time and effort spent on the project, assignment, or task.

Let us consider an assignment that requires your students to learn about tall tales in reading. Let us presume that two children are working together to find and read as many tall tales as they can to fully understand the genre. Let us also presume that they need to let the teacher and class appreciate and benefit from the knowledge they have gained from their pursuit. In order for the presentation to be academic and worthwhile, it must be well-planned in the first place and the teacher needs to meet with the students to decide the direction of the research. This, in my opinion, is where many teachers make a mistake. They don't provide enough guidance, modeling and direct teaching to help students carry on by themselves. It takes many months of directions and how-tos before we should ever let students do things on their own. Then we need to step aside and let them demonstrate how much they've learned. Once they have the skills, we need to see how far they can proceed on their own with no interference from us. As the end of the assignment we need to allow time for the celebration of the learning they will then demonstrate. This gradual release of responsibility from the teacher to the student follows the very important growing up procedures followed by good parents. First we model the learning we want them to follow, then we let them try it on their own—allowing them to put their own spin on it and carry it as far as they can.

A. Let us return to the assignment of the tall tales and see if we can adapt the points discussed above.

1. Teacher reads her curriculum guide and determines if she will be teaching tall tales, legends, myths, etc.

2. Teacher writes objectives and plans for modeling strategies that students will need to learn to understand this genre (note taking, characteristics of this type of story research techniques, and so on).

3. Teacher lets students pick a particular part of the assignment to pursue (either with a partner, small group, or alone).

4. The students work on their own for a specified period of time on the assignment with the teacher acting as a guide.

5. The students present their findings in whatever form they choose as a celebration of that learning.

B. Teachers can choose to celebrate each day, each week, each month. Be sure, however, not to make the celebrations too long and too often as they become trite and devalue the activity. Be sure as well that the activity is worthy of celebration. They can celebrate:

1. Daily assignments.

2. Units of study.

3. The end of a theme.

4. Applications of strategies.

5. A newly learned skill.

The important thing is to make sure it is something worth learning and sets a high standard of excellence. Be sure students understand its importance and connection to other concepts you will pursue. And learn to give enough guidance to allow them to enrich their learning by carrying it further than you expected. Enthusiasm for learning comes from being sure of the criteria for doing something and then putting your own style and signature on it.

II. What are portfolios? How can they be used as meaningful and purposeful assessment tools?

Paulson and Paulson (1991) offer a substantive definition of portfolio assessment:

A purposeful, integrated collection of student work showing student effort, progress, or achievement in one or more areas. The collection is guided by performance standards and includes evidence of students' self-reflection and participation in setting the focus, selecting contents, and judging merit. (p. 295)

Many teachers keep folders of student work. The key is making these portfolios meaningful and purposeful assessment tools for students, teachers and parents, as opposed to simply scrapbooks of student work.

When portfolios are used well, students place greater value and demonstrate pride in their work. They reflect, self-assess, and monitor their progress. They are held accountable for their learning progress, becoming responsible for and "owning" their learning. And a communication link is established between student, parents and teachers. The more a student is involved in creating his or her own portfolio, the more meaningful it will be.

One of the best audiences for portfolios are parents during student-led conferences.

III. What are student-led conferences?

As an adult, how would you feel if your parent or spouse went to your job evaluation and came home to tell you what your employer had to say? Would it bother you if they discussed a problem with your job performance and you weren't there to defend yourself? What if your parent or spouse forgot to tell them about that special project you were working on? Chances are you would feel out of control and powerless in your position, yet this is the position we put our students in during parent-teacher conferences.

We need to put students in charge of their own learning. This chapter is devoted to assisting you in empowering your students to develop their own portfolios and lead their own conferences. Believe it or not, with your help, your students can lead better parent conferences than you can. After all, who knows more about them than they do?

This is a real-life skill. Many colleges and businesses are requiring potential students and employees to submit a portfolio of their work and accomplishments. They also expect them to present themselves in a confident and competent manner. Just think of how impressive our students would be if they started practicing these important skills in elementary school.

Designing a portfolio and leading one's own parent-teacher conference is not only a real-life skill, but a wonderful celebration of learning for students, parents, and teachers.

According to Potter (1992), "Traditionally, during conferences, parents and teachers have met to discuss their childrens' progress for 20 minutes, approximately twice a year, and parents have had to go home and tell their children what the teacher said. In this case, the parents and the teachers assumed about 90% ownership of all accomplishments and failures of their children. If there was a problem, it was up to the parent and/or the teacher to figure out what to do about it.

In student-led conferences, students take ownership of their work, accomplishments, and plans for remediation or improvement. They spend a lot of time choosing items to go into their "professional portfolios" which are good representations of what they can do. They reflect on their learning, making notes about what they've learned, what they're especially good at, how they can apply it to daily-life situations, what they need to continue to work on, and how they plan to improve.

"The teacher plays an important and often difficult role by providing them with the knowledge and strategies which allow them to be sufficient on the day of the conference. They are there for encouragement and support only."

"The object of teaching a child is to enable him to get along without his teacher."
—Elbert Hubbard

Students design their own portfolios, according to certain guidelines (either created by the teacher or the teacher and the class). They practice their conferences with peers and anyone who will listen. When the time comes, they schedule their conferences with the teacher and invite their parents to attend. During this time, they present their portfolios to their parents using prewritten scripts and prompts.

One of the most amazing and wonderful things is seeing your students metamorphosize from the "kids" you see in class and on the playground into these incredibly professional students, who own their learning and are communicating so competently about themselves and their school performance. It never fails to give teachers and parents goose bumps!

IV. How can I teach my students to design their own portfolios, self-reflect, self- and peer-assess, take ownership of their work and accomplishments, and communicate with parents, peers, and others about their learning by leading their own conferences?

A. Inform your principal, parents, students, and other stakeholders. You can start by informing your principal, students, parents, and any other stakeholders that your students will be leading their own conferences at the end of the term. This may be difficult for some people to accept, because traditional conferences have been taking place since the beginning of time.

"It is easier to move a cemetery than to affect a change in curriculum."
—Woodrow Wilson

Good old Woodrow, what a sense of humor! Luckily, you aren't the first person to try this; it has been done successfully across the United States and Canada. If you have your principal's support, full steam ahead! The end result is worth it.

Be sure to keep everyone informed as you go, so it isn't such a mystery. Put little notes in your weekly newsletters to parents about your progress and preparations, what to expect, how to react by asking questions and showing interest, and so on. (See Figure 8–1) Give copies to your principal. After the first conference, word will get around and people will be looking forward to participating in these conferences. You won't have to work half as hard at communicating, because people will know what to expect.

Let your students know that you will do everything you can to help them be successful during their conferences, but in the end, they will be in charge. You'll show them how to develop work folders, reflect, write scripts, design portfolios, and practice for the big day. Give them a "vision" of what they will be doing at the conference. Shelly Potter (1992) tells her students, "You will dress up, because you're the professional. You'll introduce me to your parents, pick up your portfolio, and guide your parents to a table. You'll show your parents your work in each subject, discuss what you've learned, what

Dear Parents,

This fall your child will be keeping a working folder/portfolio. Traditionally, all papers have been sent home on a weekly basis. This year, the children and I will be choosing items to put into their portfolios which are kept at school. This collection will be shared with you at conference time.

In this work folder/portfolio, students take ownership of their work and accomplishments, and reflect upon their learning. These reflections make them more aware of what they've learned, what they're especially good at, and what they need to work on.

Portfolios have been very successful in many parts of the United States and Canada, and we look forward to using them in Northville. This involvement of your child in his/her learning will be beneficial in future educational and real-life situations.

We look forward to sharing these portfolios with you.

Sincerely,

FIGURE 8–1
Second-Grade
Families

you're good at, how you can apply what you've learned to daily-life situations, what you need to continue to work on, and how you plan to improve. This is also your chance to tell your parents how they can help you, and thank them for any support they've already given you. At the end, you'll thank them for coming, and either wait outside or at the table while I make any necessary closing comments and answer questions."

B. Build work folders. This is an important step in the process of building portfolios. Students and teachers place potential portfolio items into a work folder, and when it gets closer to conference time, they choose a few items per subject to go into the portfolios. This folder gives the student and teacher a wide variety of items to choose from. If one starts by placing everything directly into the portfolios, they will be so large that it will take hours to go through them. It is much more effective to work with a few key pieces per subject.

One way to store these work folders is to place them in a crate on one's counter. Each student has a hanging file with their name on it and a folder with their name on it. Thereby, when they take their folders out, they know where to put them back when they're finished. There is a date stamp and a pencil sitting beside the crate because each item in the work folder must be dated.

Students are allowed to put things in their work folders during scheduled times or during times when the rest of the class won't be interrupted. Teachers and students should discuss when the most appropriate times would be.

Keeping the student-led conference in mind, we want students to look for examples of their best work and samples of work that show growth or improvement over time. Artists and craftsmen have displayed their talents and work in portfolios for many years. Like them, we want our students to celebrate their accomplishments by demonstrating what they've learned in a positive way. We brainstorm possible items for the work folders and hang our brainstorm near the work folders where we can add to it and look at it for reminders.

Remind students that they need to include at least one item for each subject per week. This usually isn't a problem for most students, because they are very concerned about being prepared for their conferences, but one may still need to keep tabs on a few students just to make sure they are keeping up with things. A tally sheet with each subject represented is often helpful. Some teachers also require projects, pieces that show process, and certain finished products to be placed into the work folders. If you're really "hi-tech" you can include video tapes or computer discs and have a VCR or computer available during the conferences.

Students can be required to reflect on each piece as they place them into the work folders, or teachers can give students time each week to reflect on the items placed into their folders during the past week. Students realize that we take time for things that are important to us, so be sure to take the time for reflection, it is a key element in developing meaningful portfolios.

C. Teach students to self-reflect. Time for self-reflection, corrections and projections should be built into one's weekly schedule. Once a week, hand out work folders and self-adhesive notes to each student. Give them a list of prompts to choose from, and they can reflect on each piece they put into their work folders during the past week. Therefore, each piece of work in the work folders has a reflection on it. These "Prompts for Lingering Over Learning" (Potter, 1992) would include:

1. The best part about this is . . .

2. I can use this in daily-life situations when I . . .

3. Next time I do this I will be sure to . . .

Encourage your students to use different prompts as often as possible.

Primary students can check off or circle items from a list of reflective statements (see Figure 8–2), or use happy and sad faces to reflect on what they've done or learned (see Figure 8–3 and Figure 8–4).

Students can also keep weekly time planners. This is a real-life skill. They see their parents, teachers, and other professionals keep appointment books, calendars, and time planners. Now they have them, too. The best part about the student time planners is they have weekly reflections at the bottom. Their only homework on Fridays is to do their Time Planner Reflections. (see Figure 8.5). These weekly reflections are very similar to the reflections students use for their conferences. (Potter, 1992)

Once a week, collect the time planner reflections, go over them, write notes on them, and hand them back to the students. Students learn from one another as they meet to share them and analyze elements of good reflections. It is amazing how much students improve as time goes on. If you only ask them to self-

Name: _____   Date: _____

1. After writing my story I feel:

2. I have improved in:

_____ writing complete sentences

_____ using capital letters

_____ using a period at the end of a sentence

_____ spelling

_____ describing things

_____ handwriting

I am the most proud of _____

_____

_____

Next time I write, I will try to _____

_____

FIGURE 8–2
Writing Reflections

1. I feel like this when I'm not at school.

2. I feel like this when we read stories.

3. I feel like this when I write.

4. I feel like this when I'm at the Math center.

5. I feel like this when I'm at the Science center.

6. I feel like this when I do Art.

7. I feel like this when I'm at the Drama center.

FIGURE 8–3
School Feelings

*I put a (face) in # _____ because _____

_____

To help make it a (face) I will _____

_____

My teacher can help me with this by _____

_____

My parents can help me by _____

_____

*I put a (face) in # _____ because _____

_____

To help make it a (face) I will _____

_____

My teacher can help me with this by _____

_____

FIGURE 8–4
School Feelings
Follow-Up

My parents can help me by _____

_____

assess during conference time, their reflections are very shallow, at best.

Students also get frequent opportunities to self- and peer-assess by using rubrics and learning logs.

D. Assemble portfolios. Approximately two weeks before the conference, you will need to start spending larger amounts of time as students design their portfolios. They will need to choose a few items per subject, or project, that are good representations of their accomplishments that term. It is a good idea to determine ahead of time what topics will be represented in the portfolios. For example, you may choose general topics such as reading, language arts, science, social studies, and math. You may choose integrated themes, habits, or learning strategies such as communities, alternative forms of energy, homework habits, quality work, and cooperative learning. You may decide on just one or a combination of topics. Teachers and their students are the best judges of this. I recommend that everyone in the class use the same basic topics, to keep things organized and as simple as possible.

Some teachers are concerned about any discrepancies between the work represented in the portfolios and the grades they are still required to give on the report card. One way to balance that is to have an assignment sheet for each subject with the names of the assignments, the dates assigned, and the grades received. That way, if the portfolio work is outstanding and the student still got a "B" in that subject, the parent can see why.

After the students have chosen their pieces, and each piece has a reflection on it, they can start to design their scripts for their conferences. We design scripts to help students think about what is important and what they are going to say during their conferences. As students practice and learn throughout the years, they will become more and more independent, and rely on scripts less often. Remember, they don't become independent independently.

While writing their scripts, students may rely on prompts such as:

1. In . . . the most important thing I learned was . . .

2. I'm especially good at . . .

3. I can apply this to daily-life situations when I . . .

4. The thing I need to continue to work on the most is . . .

5. I will improve in this area by . . .

After reading their script for a certain topic, the students will go on to show evidence or pieces of work that reflect what they've said (Potter, 1992).

Students may also wish to include a table of contents and an opening note to their parents in their portfolios.

E. Practice with peers, teachers, and anyone who will listen. As with any performance, practice makes perfect. We wouldn't invite parents to a play without practicing to make sure it was going to be

FIGURE 8–5   Time Planner for the Week

Time Planner for the week of:	Name:
Things I have to do	Things I want to do

HOMEWORK	RDG. LOG (Title & Parent Sig.)
Monday	
Tuesday	
Wednesday	
Thursday	
Friday	

The most important thing I learned this week was _____

I can apply this to daily-life situations when I _____

The thing I need to continue to work on the most is _____

I will improve in this area by _____

I'm especially good at _____

I did something nice for someone when I _____

Portfolios and Student-Led Conferencing

successful. Likewise, we wouldn't invite parents to a student-led conference without practicing to make sure that each student will be successful.

Teachers are extremely busy, it would be very difficult to take the time to practice with each student unless you made appointments before and after school several weeks before the conferences. A less burdensome way would be to practice with a variety of audiences, such as peers, learning buddies in other grade levels, other teachers and personnel (secretaries, principals, librarians, custodians, lunch ladies, crossing guards, superintendents, and support staff), and anyone else who will listen. You may wish to design criteria for them to look over before practicing with your students such as: Can the student finish in the allotted amount of time (if there is one)? Does the work reflect what was written on the scripts? Is the portfolio organized according to the table of contents? and so forth. Or you may decide to simply remind them that this is a celebration of learning, and to show their interest and enthusiasm by asking positive questions and making positive comments and suggestions. The more your students practice, the more confident they will become.

F. Invite parents. Parents can sign up for conferences during Open House, or teachers can schedule them in collaboration with teachers at other grade levels. It is a nice idea and a real-life skill to have students write formal invitations to their parents for conferences. This is just another way of getting students to take ownership of their work and their conferences. It is also a great time to teach students the elements of a good letter or invitation. (see Figure 8–6).

G. Conference. In the primary grades, a student-led conference may be as simple as having a student take his or her parents from center to center showing them something they've done or learned there. For example, at the Math Center they could build an ABC pattern with manipulatives, and at the Writing Center they could read them a book and show them the book they've written that has the same pattern. Another idea is to have them share a few of their papers and do an activity with their parents. (see Figure 8–7).

In the upper grades, students can get very sophisticated by designing their portfolios, dressing up in their most professional clothes, putting on their most professional attitudes, and leading their own conferences. They role-play introducing their parents to the teacher, leading them to a table, sitting next to them, and having a very serious but enjoyable conversation with them about their learning.

H. Thank parents. A smart professional always follows up with a thank-you note. This is a very authentic way to teach students a real-life skill. Because students take this so seriously, it is amazing how professional their thank you letters can be (see Table 8–1).

I. Set goals for next time. If you are taking the time to reflect daily or weekly, students have had practice thinking about what they

FIGURE 8–6   Conference Invitation

Name: _____   Date: _____

Conference Invitation Rubric

This work is complete and of high quality.

Student Signature:_____   Peer Signature:_____

		SELF	PEER	TEACHER
CONTENT	Heading			
	Appropriate greeting			
	Body:			
	Purpose for the invitation			
	Place, date and time of the conference			
	Highlights of the conference			
	Appropriate closing			
	Signature			
MECHANICS	At least one inch margins			
	Correct spelling			
	Correct paragraphing			
	Correct use of punctuation			
	Written neatly			
	Written on presentable paper			
OTHER ITEMS				

COMMENTS:

1. You and your Kindergartner will visit our school library and you can help your child pick a book for this week.

2. Find a place at one of the tables to go over your child's portfolio. Let your child explain as many of the entries as s/he can, and be sure to show your interest by asking questions and making positive comments.

3. Notice the sheet entitled "My favorite learning place" and fill in the blank area with why your child likes that area of the classroom for learning.

4. Borrow the Polaroid camera, and take your child's picture in his or her favorite place. Attach the picture to the space on the "My favorite learning place" sheet.

FIGURE 8–7
Welcome to
Portfolio Day!

5. Bring your child back to class.

Thank You!!!

TABLE 8–1   Thank-You Letter

                                                      Midvale Elementary
                                                      2121 Midvale
                                                      Birmingham, Michigan 48009

Dear Mom and Dad

    Thank you for attending my conference and seeing my work. Thank you for paying special attention when I was showing you The Phantom. Your support and confidence has really helped me this year. Your understanding and concern about how I was doing in school helped me a lot. Your input and comments on my math made me proud. I look forward to doing this again.

                                                      Love,

                                                      Damien

---

need to continue to work on, setting goals and making plans for improvement. They continue to grow in their sophistication as they practice and share their goals with one another.

It helps to discuss with your students what the elements of good goals are, and as students are sharing their goals with the class they can help each other with them, or point out their strengths.

Goals are:

1. Personal—they should be designed with your needs in mind.

2. Achievable—they should be realistic and something you can actually do.

3. Observable—you should be able to see a change taking place.

4. Measurable—you can tell if you've accomplished it or not.

In the beginning of the year, a second grader wrote that her goal in math was "to do good in math." In the middle of the year, she was more specific. Her goal in math was "to get more better at take away." A sixth grader wrote that his goal in writing was "to write at least one fiction and one nonfiction book that term."

REFERENCES

Pappas, Christine C.; Kiefer, Barbara Z.; and Levstik, Linda S. *An Integrated Language Perspective in the Elementary School: Theory into Action.* White Plains, NY: Longman, 1990, pp. 320–325.

Paulson, P. R., and Paulson, F. L. *Portfolios: Stories of Knowing.* In: P. Dreyer (ed.), *Knowing: The Power of Stories,* pp. 294–303. Claremont Reading Conference, Claremont, CA, 1991.

Potter, Shelly A. *Portfolios and Student-Led Conferencing.* Birmingham, MI: The Potter Press, 1992.

Routman, Regie. *Invitations: Changing as Teachers and Learners K–12.* Toronto, Canada: Irwin; Portsmouth, NH: Heinemann, 1996.

CHAPTER 9

Community Schools and Partnerships

PHILOSOPHY

One of the newest trends in education today is establishing a school that serves as a community of learners who work on real life skills and problems, as well as academic tasks. They form partnerships with businesses and the community to solve problems encountered in the real world.

In this chapter we will discuss some experiences of schools in various parts of the country who are attempting to change their schools and are employing some exciting, new ideas and strategies, designed to motivate and energize their students.

LEARNING PRINCIPLES

Principle 7—*Characteristics of Motivation — Enhancing Learning Tasks.* Curiosity, creativity, and higher-order thinking processes are stimulated by relevant, authentic learning tasks of optimal difficulty, challenge, and novelty for each student.

Principle 9—*Social and Cultural Diversity.* Learning is facilitated by social interactions and communication with others in a variety of flexible, diverse (cross-age, cultural, family background), and adaptive, instructional settings.

The questions we will address are as follows:

I. How can I help my school to become a community of learners?

II. How do I go about creating or establishing partnerships?

III. What are the various partnerships I could try, and most importantly, how do I make sure there is a connection to learning?

I. How can I help my school to become a community of learners?

In order to help you understand how a school begins this process, I would like to describe to you a school with which I am familiar and the steps it took toward becoming a community of learners.

In the late 1980s at Midvale School in Birmingham, Michigan the staff and principal, Helen Burz, met to discuss the idea of forming partnerships with some businesses in the community. The impetus was to build a community of learners who would integrate the academic core curriculum with real-life skills and problems to be solved, by creating branches of those businesses within the school building.

The teachers and principal would identify specific skills, procedures, strategies, and enrichment taken from the core curriculum. Then they would create those learning situations within the scope of the business. The students would be responsible for running the business and solving any problems or overcoming obstacles, as you would do in conducting a real-life business. The partnership within the school would be the first endeavor of this kind in the school.

A. The Bank Connection

The discussion of forming a bank partnership grew out of the students constructing budgets in math class in Shannon Ross's fifth-grade class. She and the community organizer in the school got together to explore this idea. The community organizer, Sue Reepmeyer, contacted a nearby Michigan National Bank branch manager, David Redman, to further discuss and plan this endeavor. The following timeline evolved:

April 15, 1991—Midvale's community school organizer contacted a nearby Michigan National Bank branch manager. Together they determined that both Midvale and the bank branch were enthusiastic about opening a student-run bank in our school. The branch manager, a member of a school/business partnership committee sponsored by Birmingham Public Schools, Bloomfield Hills Schools, and the Birmingham-Bloomfield Chamber of Commerce, shared packets on existing student-run banks. Initially, many useful ideas originated from these packets.*

August 26, 1991—First planning meeting between bank staff (branch manager, assistant manager) and school staff (principal, media specialist, fifth-grade teachers, community school organizer). Together we established the following timeline and then updated it in December.

September 6, 1991—Letter sent home to fifth-grade parents explaining the plan for the bank.

September 10, 1991—Fifth-grade students tour Michigan National Bank branch.

September 13, 1991—Fifth-grade students choose a name for their bank—First Bank of Midvale.

**TABLE 9–1
Timeline**

September 17 and 24, 1991—Branch manager conducts training for all fifth graders on how to run a bank successfully, including an introduction to teller training.

(Cont.)

September 24, 1991—Job applications sent home with all fifth graders.

September 26, 1991—Job applications due to classroom teachers.

September 30, 1991—Interviews and hiring of eleven employees.

October 1 and 8, 1991—Additional training for student employees of First Bank of Midvale.

October 8, 1991—Bank structure completed for the lobby.

October 15, 1991—Grand opening and first day of banking for fifth graders.

November 13, 1991—First day of banking for fourth graders.

January 6, 1992—Job applications for new set of employees available in classroom.

January 7, 1992—First day of banking for third grade.

January 10, 1992—Job applications due. Current employees may not apply.

January 17–22, 1992—Interviews and hiring of sixteen new employees.

February 3 and 10, 1992—Training dates for new employees.

February 25, 1992—First banking day with new employees.

March 12, 1992—First banking day for second grade.

March 26, 1992—First banking day for first grade.

April 9, 1992—First banking day for kindergarten.

May 4, 1992—All-school assembly with Mr. Robert Mylod, Chairman of Michigan National Corp.

May 28, 1992—Last banking day for the school year.

TABLE 9–1
(Cont.)

*Amerman Elementary, Northville Michigan Public Schools/Community Federal Credit Union, Ling Elementary, Hemlock Michigan Public Schools/Heritage Federal Savings Bank.

The most important concern that the teachers, Shannon Ross and Joan Ferguson, felt was the learning that would result from implementing this project. It was a very time-consuming idea and needed to be shown to contain a return academically to the students. So they brainstormed with the students and each other about the curriculum goals and subjects they would integrate into the running of the bank. From this, the outline in Table 9–2 was composed:

B. Features of the Bank

1. The bank is student-run and the students are treated as employees. A bank staff employee oversees the operation.

2. The students deposit and withdraw funds as they would do at any bank branch.

3. The banking hours are determined by the staff bank personnel and students.

4. The banking, according to regulations, is for students only.

5. The fifth-grade students are the bank employees and they run the bank. All other students are potential customers.

The classroom teacher is the most important part of this partnership after it has been formed. If it is not carefully thought out it can become a burden and will not succeed because a tremendous amount of planning and implementation goes into a venture such as this. Although the goal is to ultimately have the students assume the major responsibilities, the adults are a very essential part of the program.

The major goal is to integrate the academics into the program. With this purpose in mind the following subjects were used.

Cooperative learning

1. Identified needs to form a bank
2. Communicated ideas
3. Participated in group activities

Bank functions

1. Instructional lessons: credits, debits, deposits, withdrawals
2. Internal operations of a bank

Oral communication

1. Using the telephone to solicit donations for: building a bank, lumber, paint, carpeting; obtaining materials for a grand opening, guest book, paper goods, refreshments, balloons and decorations; contacting media for coverage of the event
2. Interviewed for a position with the bank
3. Gave speeches
4. Gave presentations to other classes to encourage other classes to participate in our savings program

Written communications

1. Letter writing: media, parents, staff, Board of Education, follow-up to telephone conversations, government officials
2. Invitations
3. Thank-you notes
4. Filled out job applications
5. Letters accepting jobs
6. Wrote scripts
7. Press releases

Technology

1. Computer
2. Still photography
3. Video camera

Creativity

1. Slogans
2. Posters
3. Flyers
4. Banners

TABLE 9–2
Curriculum   There is constant evaluation and change.

6. The bank is a permanent wooden structure designed and constructed by parent volunteers with considerable input by students. It is located in the front lobby of the school.

7. The individual account ledgers are recorded and kept at the main branch of the bank, but the students have their own passbooks. The First Bank of Midvale has one overall account at Michigan National Bank.

8. Quarterly interest is paid on each student's account at the current rate.

9. A complete turnover of employees each month allows every student who chooses to participate to do so.

10. All students will be asked to open accounts by the end of the first school year. It will go according to grade: fifth graders first, then fourth, third, second, first, and kindergartners.

11. All accounts, with the exception of graduating fifth graders, will be carried over the summer in anticipation of fall banking.

C. Hiring and Training

1. The first step in becoming employees of the bank was to send a letter home written by the fifth-grade teachers and the community organizer explaining the concept and announcing a field trip to the bank.

2. The field trip included a tour of the vault and the teller area and an informal presentation by bank personnel on how a bank works and how the computer system operates.

3. Two hour-long sessions conducted by the bank personnel followed at Midvale School. The purpose of these sessions was to familiarize all the students with the responsibilities of the various positions before any hiring took place.

4. Job applications for the positions of president, branch manager (2), assistant manager (2), tellers (4), and public relations managers (2) were sent home with students. Fifteen-minute interviews were then conducted with the students who applied. Michigan National Bank employees were responsible for the interviews and at the conclusion of them, jobs were offered to those whom they chose.

5. Employees were then trained specifically for their jobs in two more hour-long sessions conducted by the bank personnel. In addition, the branch manager returned to Midvale to work with the public relations officers as they prepared to expand the operations at the school.

6. The marketing and public relations activities, such as encouraging opening of new accounts, letters to TV channels, radio stations, newspaper columnists, thank-you notes, meetings regarding process, and so on are facilitated by the fifth-grade teachers.

7. Changes in procedure, jobs, and new employee hiring and training was done in January for the remainder of the year. Staff was increased from two tellers to six and three marketing directors were hired to assist the public relations directors.

8. Job descriptions were rewritten based on the experiences of three months of banking in the school.

TITLE: Bank President

RESPONSIBILITIES AND DUTIES:

1. Supervises Branch Managers, Assistant Managers, Tellers, Marketing Directors, and Public Relations Officers

2. Responsible for overseeing the entire banking day

3. Makes sure that everyone maintains a professional image and everything runs smoothly

4. Holds regular meetings to discuss the operation of the bank and the marketing of the bank

5. Prepares the bank deposit

6. Works with Marketing and Public Relations on newsletter

7. Maintains a professional image

TITLE: Teller

RESPONSIBILITIES AND DUTIES:

1. Processes deposits and withdrawals according to bank procedure

2. Makes sure that all transactions balance

3. Balances at the end of each banking day by following set procedures

4. Operates a calculator

5. Refers customer to appropriate bank employee for assistance or account information

6. Observes all security measures

7. Maintains a professional image

TITLE: Marketing Director

RESPONSIBILITIES AND DUTIES:

1. Prepares advertisements to promote the bank

2. Works with Public Relations on newsletter

TABLE 9–3 3. Works directly with Bank President on maintaining the bank image

Job Descriptions 4. Maintains a professional image

(Cont.)

TITLE: Branch Manager

RESPONSIBILITIES AND DUTIES:

1. Prepares for banking day (the day before)

    a. makes sure there are enough deposit slips and cash-in tickets

    b. checks office for new accounts and withdrawals

    c. calls Michigan National Bank if supplies are needed or if there are any withdrawals

2. Maintains customer ledger

    a. logs deposits and withdrawals to customers' accounts

    b. helps prepare bank statements

    c. posts interest to customers' accounts

3. Will supervise the Tellers and Assistant Managers

4. Maintains order and quit during banking hours

5. Assists customers with their transactions or any questions about the bank; GIVES QUALITY CUSTOMER SERVICE

7. Assists teller with problems or difficult transactions

7. Maintains a professional image

8. Performs other employees duties when needed

TITLE: Assistant Branch Manager

RESPONSIBILITIES AND DUTIES:

1. Prepares for banking day (that morning)

    a. brings file box to the bank

    b. sets out deposit slips and pens

    c. Sets up table

2. Opens bank accounts

    a. prepares passbooks

    b. makes sure signature cards are completed correctly

    c. prepares ledger cards

    d. files signature cards and ledger cards

3. Supervises the Tellers

4. Maintains order and quiet during banking hours

5. Assists customers with transactions or any questions about the bank; GIVES QUALITY CUSTOMER SERVICE

6. Assists tellers with problems or difficult transactions

7. Performs teller job when called upon

TABLE 9–3
(Cont.)

8. Maintains a professional image

9. Performs other employees' duties when needed

TITLE: Public Relations Officer

RESPONSIBILITIES AND DUTIES:

1. Makes sure that the bank's image is maintained

2. Holds regular interviews with customers to find out what they like and don't like about the bank

3. Works with Marketing Directors on the Newsletter

4. Works directly with Bank President on all of the above

5. Maintains a professional image

A PROFESSIONAL IMAGE

GIRLS:

Must wear a skirt and blouse or a dress or a suit. (Do NOT buy something new just for this purpose!)

BOYS:

Must wear a shirt and tie with dress slacks. (Ditto)

TABLE 9–3
(Cont.) ABSOLUTELY NO JEANS AND NO TENNIS SHOES

(One of the frequent comments, I heard and ones expressed to me in writing about this endeavor, was to be aware that it evolves as time goes on and there must be ongoing evaluation of procedures, jobs, and responsibilities.)

D. Additional Training
   Another aspect of the business world that the students learned about was the BUSINESS BASICS CURRICULUM offered to upper elementary students by Junior Achievement. The four one-hour sessions were on management, organization, marketing, and production.

E. Banking Day Procedures

   1. The banking staff works in teams, with the president overseeing the operations every day that banking is occurring.

   2. Banking takes place every other week with three tellers, one branch manager, and one assistant manager on duty. The majority of the public relations and marketing takes place between banking days.

   3. Training and actual operation of the bank is supervised exclusively by the bank personnel.

   4. Students use actual deposit/withdrawal slips, bank books with account numbers, cash-in tickets, and so forth.

5. Accounts must be opened prior to banking days and a parent's signature is required, as is a social security number. A parent's signature is also required to withdraw money from any account.

F. Grand Opening of the First Bank of Midvale
   The grand opening of the First Bank of Midvale was indeed a grand affair. The students and particularly the teachers began planning for it from the day of its conception early in the fall.

G. Planning, Scheduling, and Activities

   1. Students designed the structure and an architect dad from the community created plans for it from the students' design.

   2. Another dad with experience in building cabinets built the structure and the students helped paint it.

   3. The students contacted local businesses to ask for donations of paint, carpet, and building supplies.

   4. A date was set for the opening ceremonies, coordinating with schedules in and out of school.

   5. The students wrote invitations on the computer from a guest list including such dignitaries as the President of the United States, George Bush, and the Governor of Michigan, John Engler, along with prominent local people such as city officials, TV, radio, and newspaper columnists. The superintendent of schools, John Hoeffler, and members of the Board of Education, school administration, and parents were also invited.

   6. The students not only wrote to these people but also followed up with phone calls to them.

   7. Posters were designed and the student officers of the bank visited a Board of Education meeting to share their progress.

   8. Other students met with and answered questions from the local newspapers and were interviewed for television news.

   9. A mom, who caters professionally, provided trays of sweets for the opening as well as many other moms who baked and helped coordinate the festivities.

   10. Advertising executives, public relations experts, and a stockbroker visited the classrooms to help the students plan their bank effectively.

   11. The ceremony took place in the school lobby, on October 15, 1991. The decorations were splendid, featuring red, white, and blue balloons, crepe paper, and posters. All fifth graders, their teachers, Shannon Ross and Joan Ferguson, and local school, bank, and community officials, parents, and students attended.

   12. The event was covered by three television stations, and several radio and newspaper reporters. Grades K–4 were given a tour of the bank later in the day.

13. The students spent many more days following the opening running the bank and writing numerous thank-you notes to all the people who attended and worked so hard to make it a success.

14. The teachers, school organizer, and bank personnel as well as the principal, parent volunteers, the school secretary and aide, custodial staff, and others too numerous to mention, spent many hours of their own time, energy, talent, and expertise to make this a rewarding, unique, and exciting learning experience for the students.

Following are just a few of the many forms, letters, pictures, and procedures that were so graciously allowed to be shared with you by the Midvale staff and community.

II. How do I go about creating or establishing partnerships?

In the fall of 1992, another partnership, a Post Office, was formed at Midvale School. This time it was the fourth graders who were involved. Shelly Potter and Suzanne Ostrowski were the teachers at the time.[2] Shortly after the Post Office, a School Store was opened as well.

The U.S. Federal Post Office encourages people to open post offices in schools by providing a kit. The service is called Wee Deliver. The local post office supplies sorting boxes, drop boxes, information, and personnel to aid you in establishing a school postal service.

The teachers felt that this was a way to have their students really experience an authentic business situation. They would encounter many opportunities to use reading and writing skills in a work setting, as well as integrating other subject areas such as math, science, and social studies.

A. Rationale for Opening a Post Office

1. Postal technology affects communication in the world.

2. Communication affects relationships.

3. Communication expands into the school environment.

4. The students will be able to:

(a) examine and analyze components of operating a business.

(b) develop, organize, and establish a place of business.

(c) teach significant competencies to others.

B. What They Did

1. Conducted surveys at school, took field trips to the Post Office and interviewed experts.

2. Applied for jobs, established roles, interviewed for positions, researched Post Offices, consulted with peers, high school students, teachers, and experts.

3. Collaborated with the Birmingham Post Office, carpenters who built their structure, businesses, parents, and other sources.

FIGURE 9–1 Job Application

FIRST BANK OF MIDVALE
Job Application
School Year 1991–1992

POSITION APPLYING FOR: (You may check more than one)

___ Teller   ___ Assistant Manager   ___ Branch Manager

___ Public Relations   ___ Bank President   ___ Marketing

PLEASE PRINT APPLICATION. FILL IT OUT CAREFULLY AND COMPLETELY.

Name in full _____
                 LAST   FIRST   MIDDLE

Home address _____

City & State _____ Zip _____

Home phone _____ Social Security No. _____

WORK EXPERIENCE (mowing lawns, babysitting, dishes, cleaning room)

_____

_____

_____

OTHER INFORMATION AND ACTIVITIES (sports, hobbies, awards, school activities)

_____

_____

_____

WHY ARE YOU APPLYING FOR THIS/THESE POSITIONS?

_____

_____

_____

_____

OVER

FIGURE 9–1   *(Cont.)*

Fill in this savings account book with the transactions listed here.

DATE	TYPE OF TRANSACTION	AMOUNT
1– 2–91	Deposit	20.00
1–15–91	Withdrawal	7.50
1–30–91	Interest paid	.06
2– 9–91	Deposit	11.00
2–28–91	Withdrawal	8.00
3–17–91	Deposit	9.75
3–30–91	Interest paid	.07

Account # _____

Student name _____

DATE	WITHDRAWAL	DEPOSIT	INTEREST	BALANCE

Answer these questions:

1. When do you need to use a CASH-IN ticket?   a. When you get cash
                                                b. When you get a check

2. What is a CREDIT?   a. A withdrawal slip
                        b. A deposit slip

3. What is DEBIT?   a. Cash   b. A check
                     c. A withdrawal slip   d. All of the above

We have read the attached information and understand the time and responsibilities involved if selected for a banking position.

Student's signature: _____

Parent's signature: _____

Interviewer's Comments and Recommendations: _____
_____
_____
_____
_____
_____
_____
_____
_____

FIGURE 9–2 Opening a Savings Account

FIRST BANK OF MIDVALE

2121 Midvale Street
Birmingham, Michigan 48009

INSTRUCTIONS FOR OPENING A SAVINGS ACCOUNT

Please return the attached card to the classroom teacher

on or before _____ .

To open accounts we are using cards provided by the bank
titled Request for Taxpayer Identification Number. Please fill
in these spaces only:

　　　　Student's Name
　　　　Address
　　　　Social Security Number*** (on line titled Account Number)
　　　　Student's Signature (on front)
　　　　Parent's Signature (on back)

***Please note that a social security number is <u>required</u> to open
　　an account. It will become the student's account number.

FORM W-9　　**REQUEST FOR TAXPAYER IDENTIFICATION NUMBER**

Please read the "Request for Taxpayer Identification Number Instructions" before completing this form. In order to be valid, the form must be signed and dated, and must contain your correct taxpayer identification number.

NAME	TAX IDENTIFICATION NUMBER
STREET ADDRESS	ACCOUNT NUMBER
CITY　　STATE　　ZIP CODE	TYPE OF ACCOUNT
BANK OF ACCOUNT	BRANCH

☐ Under penalties of perjury I certify (1) that the number shown on this form is my correct taxpayer identification number and (2) that I am not subject to back-up withholding either because I have not been notified that I am subject to back-up withholding as a result of a failure to report all interest or dividends, or the Internal Revenue Service has notified me that I am no longer subject to back-up withholding. **(NOTE:** If you have been notified by the Internal Revenue Service that you are subject to back-up withholding and have not been notified that back-up withholding has been terminated, then you must strike out clause (2) above. **)**

☐ I (we) qualify for exemption from withholding on interest and dividends under one or more of the definitions of exempt recipient as set forth in the "Request for Taxpayer Identification Number Instructions."

SEE REVERSE FOR "APPLIED FOR" DECLARATION

Signature _____　Date _____
14046 (1/84)

FIGURE 9–3 Teller Report

Teller Report

Cash Count

50's = ¢ ___ . FIFTIES

20's = $ ___ . TWENTIE

10's = $ ___ . TENS

5's = $ ___ . FIVES

2's = $ ___ . TWO

1's = $ ___ . ONES

Coin

$1.00 = ___ . DOLLARS

.50¢ = ___ . HALVES

.25¢ = ___ . QUARTER

.10¢ = ___ . DIMES

.05¢ = ___ . NICKELS

.01¢ = ___ . PENNIES

Total ___ $

starting cash – ___ .

Cash·in's – ___ .

Withdrawals – ___ .

Ending Cash – ___ .

Total (s/b 0) ___ .

NAME

DATE

1st BANK OF MIDVALE
SAVINGS DEPOSIT/WITHDRAWAL

NAME	DATE

AMOUNT WITHDRAWN $_____

CASH	
COIN	
CHECK(S)	
TOTAL	

STUDENT'S SIGNATURE

PARENT OR GUARDIAN SIGNATURE

ACCOUNT NUMBER

– – – – – – – – – –

FIGURE 9–4
Fifth Grader
Oversees Operations

4. Contacted an Eagle Scout that was looking for a community project he needed to complete for his scouting requirements.

5. Defined job roles, devised accounting and ordering systems, and consulted experts.

6. Used computer desk top publishing and the writing process to create ads, contests, skits, speeches, letters, and fliers.

An open house advertising their Post Office was held in the spring of 1993 and the students planned and executed it all themselves with minimal help from the teachers. The superintendent and deputy superintendent attended the ceremony along with the local postmaster, post office personnel, and parents in the community.

The students demonstrated their project through the use of speeches, computer advertisements, slide shop, visual aid skits, and a rap song they created. It was a very successful affair in which they were rightfully proud. And the best part was the real life experiences they gained.

An outgrowth of this experience was a stationery store. The students saw a need for designing stationery to encourage use of the Post Office. They designed personal notes, cards, and sheets by using the students' school pictures. This did create more interest in the Post Office and led them on to opening a School Store to sell their stationery and other supplies. They started with shares and sold them to shareholders for a dollar. At the end of the year the shares sold for a dollar and a half.

III. What are the various partnerships I could try, and most importantly, how do I make sure there is a connection to learning?

One of the outcomes of starting a business and forming a partnership of some kind is it leads to more and more authentic involvement with the community. Many cities have community organizers at the school that promote this idea. An outgrowth of this can be an actual town of businesses. This is what occurred at Midvale. The principal who followed Helen Burz, Dale Truding, continued to encourage this development.

A. The town of Midvale, a child-centered community, was founded with these purposes in mind:[3]

   1. To build a community of learners that integrates core curriculum with real-life problems in a meaningful way.

   2. To have students face some obstacles that they must overcome themselves by brainstorming and experimenting with solutions to those problems, just as a real business does.

   3. Put students' learning into real-life experiences where they practice the basics of literacy, math, science, social studies, and other subjects.

   4. Encourage a cooperative spirit among students of all ages as well as adults from all walks of life.

   5. To learn first-hand from experts in the field how things are done in many different businesses.

   6. To assess learning in an ongoing way, using rubrics designed in part by the students themselves, clarifying roles procedures and skills.

   Staff members at Midvale School designed and operated the following types of businesses:

   • Baker's Batch—a business run by first graders in partnership with Townsend Bakery, an exclusive bakery in a hotel in town. They baked and sold cookies, brownies, and other goodies to the students.

   • Midrock Cafe—a business that served lunch, snacks, and drinks and employed wait staff, entertainment, and T-shirt designers.

   • Midvale Newspaper—a staff of reporters and printing personnel that worked in conjunction with the high school to put out a paper. It included news of the day, articles of interest, interviews with special people, staff, students, and community leaders as well as news of TV programs and movies.

   • WMVL 21—a multimedia organization that helped students learn to use a scanner, computerized still camera, CD-ROM, and much more to create an amazing production of any kind.

   • Midvale Historical Society—a group investigating the past history of the school. They would organize it into a book for others to read and appreciate.

   • Midvale Jump Rope Team—a school for learning the ins and outs of jump-roping skills and tricks.

- Crafty Crafts—a business teaching how to make and sell all kinds of crafts.

- Stamping—this group showed how to explore the world of rubber stamps. They learned ways to create wearable art, unique cards, and mail art to send to friends.

- Entertainment Today—a group that encouraged the creative talents in the building: disc jockeys, actresses, actors, face painters, business managers, set designers, and talent scouts.

B. Other Schools Creating School/City Environments

Some schools across the country are going beyond the concept of school/business partnerships and are creating a school that is run by the students. It is called a "microsociety" and is popular on the east coast.

The students learn math by having jobs in the school stores, they pay taxes, and own many types of businesses. They have their own money system and their own courts and laws. They write their own constitution and plan and govern all the activities and rules to live by in the school community.

The term "microsociety" originated from a man named George Richmond, an acclaimed educator who was looking for a way to reach discouraged and disillusioned youngsters living in the Brookline, Massachusetts area. He felt that since the discipline he saw was not working, perhaps giving them freedom and responsibility would. He started employing some of his ideas in his classroom and then wrote a book about his experiences.

The book helped to launch the first school based on the microsociety model. It was called City Magnet School and opened in 1981 in an empty library in Lowell, Massachusetts. Since then, the New York school districts of Yonkers and Newburgh as well as the Massachusetts district of Pepperell have created their own microsocieties.

The results of testing seem to prove that this type of education is beneficial as the scores are higher than in some traditional schools in the areas. In 1990, some eighth graders passed tests in math and reading given to first-year college students. School attendance, which had been a problem, has been higher as well and students are not dropping out of school.

Even though this type of schooling and schools may seem radical and not necessary in all areas of the country, we need to keep an open mind and try new approaches to learning. In many parts of the country we are failing to reach the youngsters and as long as we are sure that learning is taking place, we need to try alternatives.

C. Schools of Choice and Charter Schools

There are two types of schools that are in the news in the state of Michigan recently. They are called schools of choice and charter schools. I would like to describe one school of choice that opened in the fall of 1995 in Birmingham, Michigan. The principal at this school as well as some staff members were at the Midvale school of which I've written.

1. Schools of Choice

    The school will have a grade 3–8 configuration and will incorporate the following philosophy. (Birmingham Covington School (B.C.S.)).[4]

    It will offer:

    • a clear choice in educational structure.

    • a rigorous academic challenge.

    • a curriculum that emphasizes integrated learning of all subject matter.

    • an emphasis on theme development exploration.

    • inquiry and collaboration-based learning.

    • a focus on integration and application of basic skills.

    • a special emphasis on comprehensive science and technology.

    • in-depth understanding of the principles of scientific inquiry, design, and application that will lead to a more comprehensive understanding of the relationship between science and technology, history and the humanities.

    • flexible groupings that match developmental needs.

    • supportive teaching teams that collaborate, organize and deliver appropriate instruction to students.

    • mentoring opportunities inside and beyond the four walls.

    • student choice in specialization and hands-on learning.

    • a link between the classroom and the international community that encourages expanding knowledge of global issues, literature, the arts, and teaches all the students the Spanish language.

    Students applied for placement in the school and it is ready now to begin offering students a real alternative to traditional education. This is such an important concept in our world today as we approach the twenty-first century.

2. Charter Schools—What are They?

    Eleven states have passed laws permitting the creation of autonomous public schools that operate outside of the school districts' regular or traditional schools. They are funded by the state in many different ways (in Michigan funds come from the state lottery and sales taxes) and can plan their own curriculum. The 140 charter schools currently in the nation are as different from one another as they are from the traditional public schools. Some specialize in science, math, the humanities, and so forth. But they all reflect a fundamental change in education that strongly advocates in most instances, student choice, teacher empowerment, increased use of technology, and authentic evaluation that emphasizes individual and group achievement. They have a vision of what schools should be like moving into the technical, global, informational society of the twenty-first century. We know that the bureaucratic, industrial mode, public educational system we now use is not only outdated but simply is unable to meet the demands and needs of the future.

Some Features of Charter Schools

- Set their own curriculum.

- Reduce class size.

- Encourage hands-on learning.

- Increase use of technology.

- Create interdisciplinary classes.

- Emphasize individual talents.

- Promote cooperative learning.

- Collaborate with parents and community in setting goals and objectives.

Some Restrictions Imposed by States

- Number of schools allowed to operate (varies from state to state)

- Money allotted to group applying for a charter (sometimes involves public school funds, in other cases grants, lotteries, taxes, special assessments, and so forth)

- Local school board approval

- Proof of achievement (testing, observations, and so on)

- Licensed teachers

- Building codes and restrictions

- Application by lottery, testing, first-come, first-serve basis

3. Parent Involvement in Schools

One of the crucial differences in today's schools is the increased involvement of parents in the process of their child's learning. Most teachers welcome this collaboration and view it as an essential component of the change in teaching that is currently occurring.

There are many ways that parents are involved in their schools. Some ways include direct participation in the process, others are more indirect.

Let's look at some of those ways:

Direct Involvement in the Schools

- As an aid assisting with students (such as library, computer, or practice and recreational reading).

- As a clerical aid assisting the teacher with paper work.

- As a part time volunteer for field trips, fairs, projects, or other events.

- As an office aid assisting school secretaries with various tasks.

Indirect Involvement

- Through reading the school or class newspaper.

- Through attending P.T.A. or P.T.O. meetings.

- Through serving on committees.

- Through attending parent's night, conferences, school programs, fairs, and so forth.

- Through assistance in homework.

Parents are more apt to cooperate and collaborate with their child's school and teacher if they feel needed and wanted. The following ways help parents to feel that commitment.

- Keeping the parents informed regarding classroom activities, assignments, projects, and so on

- Meeting them at the beginning of the year in an informal setting (picnic, open house, or other event)

- Setting a specific plan for communication (days for work to be sent home, home visits if desirable, school visits)

- Mutual goal setting, evaluation, homework policies, and so on

- Use of school TV channel (if available) or radio to broadcast and inform parents of upcoming events

- Development of a school or class newspaper to chronicle daily events and activities, accomplishments, original poems, stories, and projects created and reported by the students themselves

- A parent handbook listing tips, helpful hints for studying, test taking, parent conferencing, doing homework, book lists, and so forth

- A school directory listing phone numbers and addresses of parents and school personnel

There may be many other specific ways to encourage involvement of parents in your school because all situations are unique and bring with them their own set of challenges and problems to solve. The important issue is that we recognize that times have changed and it is important for everyone to work together to solve the enormous changes we face in the future. Our world is expanding in ways most people have difficulty even comprehending. And our children face a changing society that we can only imagine. We must rise to the occasion and provide our youngsters with the skills, creativity, and technology to survive and flourish in that world of tomorrow. And we need to form partnerships with our parents and communities to encourage and support this change.

ENDNOTES

1. David Redman, Anne Althoff, Helen Burz, Joan Ferguson, Shannon Ross, and Susan Reepmeyer. *First Bank of Midvale, A School/Business Partnership between Midvale School, Michigan National Bank, Birmingham, Michigan* (Birmingham Public Schools Report Booklet). October, 1992.

2. Shelly Potter. *Notes, Information on Post Office*. 1992.

3. Members of Midvale School Staff. *Welcome to the Town of Midvale, A Child-Centered Community* (Booklet). 1994.

4. Dale Truding and staff. *Final Draft 3-8 Philosophy for New B.C.S., Birmingham, Michigan*. 1995.

REFERENCES

Raywid, Mary Anne. *The Struggles and Joys of Trailblazing—A Tale of Two Charter Schools*. Phi Delta Kappan, March, 1995.
Wallis, Claudia. *A Class of Their Own*. Time, October 31, 1994.

CHAPTER 10

Demonstrating Learning Using Multimedia Techniques

PHILOSOPHY

In many classrooms all across the United States we are beginning to see the use of technology to help children learn. Although many types of technology, and in particular computers, have been in use for at least the past ten years, many teachers have not incorporated technology into their daily teaching.

There are many reasons stated by teachers for not doing this:

1. Changing Technology—As soon as teachers are comfortable with a new method to use, the technology changes. Hardware and software production is changing so rapidly that almost daily some become obsolete.

2. Varying Levels of Preparation—There are so many levels of expertise in a classroom. Students' backgrounds vary considerably. In cases where the students have computers in their own homes, for instance, they sometimes know more than the teacher who may not possess a computer.

3. State Regulations—Rules regarding computer training are different from state to state, indeed, even from school district to school district within a given state. State Departments of Education and professional organizations are establishing or have established guidelines for what technology skills teachers need. In many instances, teachers have not had a course in the use of computers or other technology. And depending upon the budget of the state or in most cases the local district, money may not be available for equipment for them to use. Regulating what little technology equipment is available prevents its daily use in the classroom.

   Ten years ago the goals for teacher competencies in technology were that the teacher should:

   (a) be able to use the computer as a tool for solving problems.

   (b) have the experience of using the computer in the learning of subject matter.

    (c) have knowledge of computer vocabulary.

    (d) be able to use the computer as a tool (using applications such as word processing, spreadsheet analysis, data-based management).

    (e) be familiar with computer hardware, including everyday operation and use of a variety of machines.

Many teachers still list concerns with using computers:

1. Fear of Uncertainty—Teachers are familiar with the materials they've been using for years. Having a change in attitude that basically admits, "I don't know how this works, but I can see what it can do," is not easy for some teachers. The fear of embarrassing themselves in front of students while learning is not a comfortable situation for many. They think it undermines authority.

2. Teacher/Student Relationship—Many teachers fear that students will become so independent that they will not want to work with the teacher, but will prefer the computer. They will learn to reinforce basic skills, keep records, focus attention, simulate environments, calculate and perform many functions independent of the teacher. No matter how many of us believe this to be desirable there are many who do not. They feel that relationships change when the student knows more about the computer than the teacher. While some teachers welcome the opportunity to restructure a classroom, others are uncomfortable with this change.

3. Concerns About Accountability—How will using technology play a role in measuring teacher accountability? How do you measure or recognize work done on the computer by students?

LEARNING PRINCIPLES

Principle 5—*Motivational Influences on Learning.* The depth and breadth of information processed, and what and how much is learned and remembered, is influenced by

    (a) self-awareness and beliefs about personal control, competence, and ability.

    (b) clarity and saliency of personal values, interest, and goals.

    (c) personal expectations for success or failure.

    (d) affect, emotion, and general states of mind.

    (e) the resulting motivation to learn.

Principle 11—*Individual Differences in Learning.* Although basic principles of learning, motivation, and effective instruction apply to all learners (regardless of ethnicity, race, gender, presence or absence of physical handicaps, religion or socioeconomic status), learners differ in their preferences for learning modes and strategies and have unique capabilities in particular areas. These differences are a function of both environment (what is learned and communicated in different cultures or other social groups) and heredity (what occurs naturally as a function of genes and resulting differential capacities).

The Questions we will address in this chapter are:

I. What are some of the terms that explain the different systems in technology?

II. How do you manage and use technology in a classroom with many learning styles and a multitude of different projects occurring simultaneously?

III. How do you use the technological equipment in most elementary buildings to help students create their productions/presentations?

IV. What are the advantages of this use of technology and how do we encourage its implementation?

I. What are some of the terms that explain the different systems in technology?

Perhaps defining what multimedia instruction is and how we can use it in a classroom will help us to make the first steps toward implementation.

"Multimedia is," according to Gayeski (1993), "A class of computer-driven interactive communication systems which create, store, transmit, and retrieve textual, graphic and auditory networks of information."[1]

These terms are used to explain the different systems:

C.B.T.	Computer-based training using a mainframe or personal computer.
C.D.I.	Compact disk-interactive, a CD-ROM based self-contained system which is attached to a regular TV set.
CD-ROM	Compact disk-read only memory, a small optical disk used to store and play back digital data. It stores on one disk what is on several hundred floppy disks.
C.D.T.V.	Commodore Dynamic Total Vision, an interactive multimedia player incorporating a CD-ROM player and an Amiga computer engine that can display programs on a television monitor.
D.V.I.	Digital Video Interactive—a standard for

compression/decompression of digitized video/audio stored on a CD-ROM, digital tape, or large capacity computer hard drive by way of specialized cards.

Expert System	An interactive system that solves problems and helps users learn to document and develop a knowledge base.
Hypermedia	A classification of software programs that consists of related text, graphics, audio files, and video chips.
Hypertext	A classification of software programs that consists of networks of related text files.
I.V.D.	Interactive Videodisc, analog optical discs capable of storing and playing back 54,000 still frames or 30 minutes of motion video (per side) and two channels of audio (controlled by a remote control).
M.P.C.	Multimedia Personal Computer, a trademark for both soft and hardware systems.
P.C.V.C.R.	NEC's name for their videocassette recorder that can be controlled by a personal computer.
P.S.S.	Performance Support System, a computer-based point-of-use interactive "job aid" that helps users by giving them on-line information help on problem solving and tutorials.
Quick-Time	Apple Computer's multimedia technology that supports storage and distribution of motion video stills and audio over local area networks.
Teleconferencing	Voice or motion video by means of phones or satellite broadcasting.
Ultimedia	An IBM trademark for their multimedia hardware (personal computers with CD-ROM players, optional D.O.I. digital video capabilities).
Virtual Reality	Systems displaying and controlling synthetic scenes using computers and peripherals that sense movements such as data gloves, helmets, or joysticks.

II. How do you manage and use technology in a classroom with many learning styles and a multitude of different projects occurring simultaneously?

Whenever students are planning projects to demonstrate learning, there will be differences in how they would like to present the information. Therefore, teachers need to be aware of these differences and assist the students in their choice of technology.

The first step is to introduce your children to as many technologies as possible and either demonstrate their use yourself or have your media specialist do it for you. Get to know how your specialist can assist you at the beginning of the year and have your children do the same.

The important issue in managing a classroom with so many personalities and learning styles is to have the responsibility for the work and method of procedure rest with the students themselves. If you follow these steps, your children will learn to be independent users of many types of technology.

A. Steps to Using Technology

1. Introduce the types of technology that can be used for projects (one at a time).

2. Allow the children a lot of practice time using the technology.

3. Model the use of a particular one for a project done with the whole class.

4. Assign topics and let the students choose the type of technology (or technologies) they would like to use.

5. Allow sufficient time for them to research and plan their presentation.

6. Schedule times for presentations after meeting individually with the students in their various groups to preview their projects.

Knowing how you learn is important in establishing the method of presentation and the type of technology one might use. So, it's crucial to help students become aware of the procedure for metacognition. Most students as early as second grade are beginning to be cognizant of their strengths and can readily understand the importance of learning how they learn.

One way to do this is to make a questionnaire that will trigger an awareness of their learning style or you can use a commercial personality or learning style inventory already formulated.

III. How do you use the technological equipment in most elementary buildings to help students create their productions/presentations?

Some of the biggest obstacles to overcome in this age of technology are how to keep abreast of the latest equipment available and how to afford purchasing it for your school.

It is important to utilize what you already have in your school building as well. The first step is to inventory the various equipment available (if that has not already been done). Then you need to have an expert in the field of technology (either in your school system or outside in the business community) come in and demonstrate how you can use the various types of equipment together. The children need to be made aware of this for future productions they will want to create.

The next thing you need to do is make a plan for the year, again enlisting the assistance of the media/businessperson. Make it simple:

A. Choose hardware/software that is easy to use so that your students will feel successful.

B. Set aside time, money, and space for productions. (Ask your P.T.A. or some other parent or business group for help.)

C. Keep records of what your children use and prefer for their productions.

D. Add to the existing systems in your building rather than starting something new (even if it's a bit outdated).

E. Buy several inexpensive tools rather than some elaborate ones. It's better to buy several simpler tools for productions that excel in creating certain types of applications—such as computer-generated slide shows, tutorials, or hypertext—since no one authoring tool really does all these jobs equally well. You need to select, learn, and apply/demonstrate these tools (or again have someone do it for you).

F. Plan for reviews and updating by using periodicals and books to amplify and supplement your knowledge of multimedia/technology. There are new things on the market daily.

G. Enlist help from your media person—make her or him your best friend.

IV. What are the advantages of this use of technology and how do we encourage it's implementation?

A. Combining Use of a Videodisc and Computer
There are many pieces of equipment that can be used in the classroom that enhance learning. The combination of a videodisc (a disc on which images are stored) and a computer offers new and interesting possibilities, for example, reading aloud to children. Children could benefit in the following ways:

1. Books can be introduced in an interesting manner.

2. Children can practice listening skills.

3. They can review a book already read for extended lessons or activities.

One program available can be used on IBM Infowindow and is written in the IBM authoring language HANDY. It allows children to view a story one page at a time in a flexible and interactive way. They can view the story page by page from beginning to end or move around in the story in a random manner. There are also activities that accompany the program and children can work independently on these. Of course it's important to regard these activities in accordance with your philosophy and not necessarily do all the ones suggested. You might want to make up some of your own or even have your children try inventing some ways to use the program.

The following activities are suggested with the program:

1. Find the word—program highlights a word and the child finds the matching object in a picture and touches it.

2. Program highlights a part of the picture, and the student finds and touches the matching word in the story.

3. The student finds a word and an object that match and touches both.

4. Words on the move—a paragraph is shown on the screen with some words deleted and the child picks words to go in the blanks from a list at the bottom of the page or screen.

5. Word-Finder—A paragraph is shown with some words highlighted. Children can be asked questions having to do with the meaning of the words for practice of vocabulary or they can write stories or sentences using the words.

This is an easy program to use and can help children get used to doing some things on a computer. You need to find a lot of activities or make up a lot that will accustom your students to becoming familiar with computers and trying some creative activities of their own. (See the list of programs at the end of the chapter to try with your children.)

B. Using a Computer for Science

Another way to use a computer is to use them as "silent partners." The software is made up of microcomputer-based laboratory materials (M.B.L.) such as temperature probes, light probes, and heat pulsars for the collection of data. All these, including accompanying curriculum materials, are developed by Technical Education Research Centers in Boston. (See information at the end of the chapter.)

C. Using a Computer as a Learning Center/Station

You can establish a learning center or station in your room using a computer. Students can compose stories, solve problems in math, or experiment with software that is available. Of course, using one in these ways requires solving logistical problems such as, "Who uses it when?", "How can I divide the time equitably during the week?", "What kinds of projects/assignments warrant the use and are better accomplished on a computer?"

It's necessary to make up a schedule to ensure everyone will have equal access. (If they choose to use it.) Once or twice a week for 30 minutes, if you have only one computer, seems to be reasonable for most classrooms. (Two children can partner, so you would need to have maybe three or four thirty-minute blocks of time a day.)

You also need to establish a time when the other children are doing some independent work that allows for individual children or partners to work on a project/lesson without missing an activity in class. Children seem to enjoy working with a partner on the computer and it helps in scheduling blocks of time, as you need only 12 half hours versus 24.

It is important to decide what kinds of lessons/projects for which you want your students to use the computer(s). At the beginning of the week or whenever you write your lesson plans, it's important to think about which ones are conducive to using the computer. Rather than always using it for writing, consider it's use in other areas. Investigate the software available in your library/media center and also consult with your media specialist for suggestions.

D. Using a Computer for Interactive Demonstrations

You can program or have someone else program several whole-class lessons on the computer. Or you can get software to demonstrate uses of the computer in the areas of reading/writing, math, science, and social studies. Once children can see and interact with these various programs, they can then use them in their partnerships or small groups to research, plan, and implement projects and presentations.

E. Use of Computers with Special Education Students

Teaching special education students how to use a computer or word processor is particularly important for improving self-esteem. Many students who are disabled have difficulty producing any papers, projects, or assignments in a legible, coherent way. And so, if they are taught how to use word processing skills or computer software programs, they can be more successful. It often serves as an equalizer among the students and between them and other students in the building. Many of these students will need, as do all students, to interact with all kinds of electronic devices in their lives. So it's important to give them school experiences with computer-based technology.

F. Word Processors

Word processors have many uses in a classroom. The word processor software can be used for writing stories, making classroom books, keeping records, creating lessons in vocabulary, accessing other classmate's stories, making tests, and creating spelling lessons. The expense involved acquiring word processors is, of course, much less than purchasing computers. Spreadsheets allow teachers to use rows and columns to manipulate, classify, and categorize numbers, and words for grading, making lessons, keeping track of progress for portfolios, and so on. It can be a very useful addition to the equipment in a classroom.

G. Telecommunications

More buyers of computers are now including a modem in the purchase. It allows communication with other computer users through the telephone. It's possible in this way to access what is called bulletin boards and electronic databases. You can use the bulletin board to leave messages, peruse information, ask questions of other users, and so on. The electronic databases index and evaluate software, allow access to information from such sources as encyclopedias, newspapers, and travel agencies. Some of the following data bases are now in use:

- DIALOG

- CompuServe

- E.P.I.E.

- Online

- NASA

Note: There are many others coming on line so you need to ask and update this list continually. Ask about bulletin boards as well.

H. Advantages of Forms of Media Over Text Alone

We know that texts are good for description, explanation, compare/contrast, definition, problem/solution as well as labels, titles, and captions. Graphics in print are good for location and spatial information and can be used for temporal sequences (cycle charts): compare/contrast (histograms) and other depictions/displays. But the following uses of media forms cannot be duplicated using print.

a. Hypertext—can organize large amount of information into smaller, easier to understand chunks. It can help to make understandable how they are related and the user can utilize those small chunks in any way, any time.

b. Animation—is useful for simulating physical processes. It may also be used as an attention mechanism or for entertainment.

c. Motion Video—is a recognized, powerful tool for communication. It can be used for presentations of any kind and is useful for the modeling necessary in everything you do. Children are familiar with it's many uses because of their long exposure to TV, movies, Nintendo, and all kinds of other videos.

d. Still Photography—has many uses in a classroom to show people, places, and things. It can enhance descriptions and explanations. It can also be used to illustrate sequences or provide examples.

e. Music, Speech, Sound—make any presentation more exciting and interesting. Children are masters at weaving these mediums into productions/presentations. Most already know how to use them effectively and if given permission to do so can create wonderful audioizations.

1. Factors Affecting Use of a Selection of Media for Instruction

• Facilities	• Content
• Time	• Effective Communication
• Availability	• Reasonable Cost
• Market	• Practical Constraints
• Objectives	• Human Factors

- Learners
- Teachers

2. Trends
   - Faster computers
   - Lower cost
   - Better storage system
   - Video integration
   - Networks or Distance-Learning Set Ups
   - Improved graphics
   - Better, more appropriate, specific, user-friendly software

Teachers are beginning to use computers as they see the effects on their children. And I believe the future will include continued use of all the technology mentioned in this chapter. I also believe that long-distance learning through networking will become popular and will encourage increased use of all types of electronic multimedia.

Remember when you decide to use technology of any kind to model its use and then stand aside and let your children create their own way. Once again this is the way to empower children to be independent, motivated learners.

ENDNOTES

1. Diane M. Gayeski, ed. *Multimedia for Learning Development, Application, Evaluation* p. 4–6 (Educational Technology Publications, NJ, 1993).

REFERENCES

Congress of the United States, Office of Technology Assessment. *Power On! New Tools for Teaching and Learning*. For sale by the Superintendent of Documents, Washington DC. 20402-9325, 1988.

Dix, Don, and Spiro, Rand. *Cognition, Education, Multimedia-Exploring Ideas in High Technology*. Hillsdale, NJ: Lawrence Erlbaum Associates, Publishers, 1990.

Daiute, Collette, and Morse, Frances. Access to Knowledge and Expression: Multimedia Writing Tools for Students with Diverse Needs and Strength. *Journal of Special Education Technology,* vol. 12, n3, pp. 221–256, Spring, 1994.

Leu, Donald J., and Kinzer, Charles K. *Effective Reading Instruction K–8*. 2nd ed. New York: Macmillan, 1991, pp. 564–602.

Oliver, Ron, and Perzylo, Lesa. "Children's Information Skills: Making Effective Use of Multimedia Sources." *Education and Training Technology International,* vol. 31, n3, pp. 219–230, August, 1994.

RESOURCES

Organizations and Publications for More Information

1. Association for the Development of Computer-Based Instruction Systems, 1601 West Fifth Avenue, Suite #111, Columbus, Ohio 43212 *(Journal of Computer-Based Instruction)*

2. Association for Educational Communications and Technology, 1025 Vermont Avenue, NW., Washington, DC 20005 (Tech Trends, Educational Technology Research and Development)

3. Educational Technology Publications, Inc., 700 Palisade Avenue, Englewood Cliffs, NJ 07632 (Educational Technology)

4. International Interactive Communications Society, P.O. Box 26, Falls Church, VA 22040 (produce multimedia soft/hardware)

5. Meckler Corporation, 11 Ferry Lane West, Westport, CT 06880 (Multimedia Review)

6. Society for Applied Learning Technology, 50 Culpepper St. Warringtown, VA 22186 (Instruction Delivery Systems; *Journal of Interactive Instruction Development*)

7. Weingarten Publications, Inc. 38 Chauncey St., Boston, MA 02111 (CBT Directions)

8. LaserDisc Newsletter (provides monthly video-disc lists with critiques) Suite 428, 496 Hudson Street, N.Y., NY 10014.

Multimedia Resources

1. Arwardy, J., and Gayeski, D. *Using Video; Interactive and Linear Designs.* Englewood Cliffs, NJ: Educational Technology Publications, 1989.

2. Blattner, M. M., and Dannenberg, R. B. *Interactive Multimedia Computing.* Reading, MA. Addison-Wesley, 1992.

3. Cabeceiras, J. *The Multimedia Library: Materials Selection and Use.* Orlando, Fla.: Academic Press, 1991.

4. Hodges, M. E. (ed.) *Multimedia Computing at M.I.T.'s Project Athena.* Reading, MA.: Addison-Wesley. 1992.

5. Iuppa, N. V. *The Multimedia Adventure.* White Plains, NY. Knowledge Industry Publications, 1992.

6. Imke, S. *Interactive Video Management and Production.* Englewood Cliffs, NJ: Educational Technology Publications, 1991.

7. Kasten, A. S., Miller, R. L., Reeve, V. L., and Sayers, J. H. *Multimedia and Related Technologies: A Glossary of Terms.* Falls Church, VA: Future Systems, 1991.

8. Lamb, A. *Emerging Technologies and Instruction: Hypertext, Hypermedia, and Interactive Multimedia.* Englewood Cliffs, NJ: Educational Technology Publications, 1991 (Selected Bibliography Series, Vol. #4).-

9. Maddux, C., Johnson, D., and Willis, J. *Educational Computing: Learning with Tomorrow's Technologies.* Boston: Allyn and Bacon, 1992.

10. Schwier, R., and Misanchuk, E. U. *Interactive Multimedia Instruction.* Englewood Cliffs, N.J. Educational Technology Publications, 1993.

11. Weihs, J. *The Integrated Library: Encouraging Access to Multimedia Materials.* Phoenix, AZ: Oryx Press, 1991.

12. Wilson, S. *Mutimedia Design with Hypercard.* Englewood Cliffs, NJ: Prentice-Hall, 1991.

SOFTWARE SOURCES

1. Active Learning Systems
   5365 Avenidas Encinas Suite
   Carlsbad, CA 92008
   800-423-0818

2. Addison-Wesley
   2725 Sand Hill Road
   Menlo Park, CA 94025
   800-447-2226

3. Apple Computer, Inc.
   2525 Mariani
   Cupertino, CA 95014
   800-732-3131, ext. 254

4. Baudville
   5380 52nd Street, S.E.
   Grand Rapids, MI 49508
   616-698-0888

5. Britannica Software
   345 Fourth Street
   San Francisco, CA 94107

6. Broderbund Software
   P.O. Box 12947
   San Rafael, CA 94913-2947
   800-527-6263

7. Bytes of Learning
   150 Consumers Road, #202
   Willowdale, Ontario
   Canada M2J1P9
   416-495-9913

8. COM Press/Queue
   562 Boston Avenue
   Bridgeport, CT 06610
   800-232-2224

9. Conduit
University of Iowa
Oakdale Campus
Iowa City, IA 52242
319-335-4100

10. Davidson & Associates, Inc.
3135 Kashiwa Street
Torrence, CA 90505
800-556-6141

11. DC Heath/Collamore
P.O. Box 19309
2700 North Richard Avenue
Indianapolis, IN 46219
800-428-8071

12. DesignWare, Inc.
185 Berry Street
San Francisco, CA 94107
415-546-1866

13. Didatech Software Limited
3812 William Street
Burnaby, B.C.
Canada V5C3H9
604-299-4435

14. DLM Teaching Resources
P.O. Box 4000
One DLM Park
Allen, TX 75002
800-527-5030

15. Educational Materials and
Equipment Corporation
P.O. Box 2805
Danbury, CT 06813-2805
800-848-2050

16. Edu.SOFT
P.O. Box 2560
Berkeley, CA 94702
800-EDU-SOFT

17. Focus Media
839 Stewart Avenue
P.O. Box 865
Garden City, NY 11530
800-645-8989

18. Gessler Publishing Co.
900 Broadway
New York, NY 10003
212-673-3113

19. Grolier Electronic Pub. Inc.
95 Madison Ave., Suite 1100
New York, NY 10016
212-696-9750

20. High Technology Software
Products
8200 N. Classen Blvd., #101
Oklahoma City, OK 73114
405-848-0480

21. Holt, Rinehart & Winston
383 Madison Avenue
New York, NY 10017
212-872-2000

22. HRM - Queue
562 Boston Avenue
Bridgeport, CT 06610
800-232-2224

23. IBM Direct Response
Marketing, Dept. TR
101 Paragon Drive
Montvale, NJ 07645
800-IBM-2468 ext. 900TR

24. The Learning Co.
6493 Kaiser Drive
Fremont, CA 94555
800-852-2255

25. Logo Computer Systems
121 Mt. Vernon Street
Boston, MA 02108
800-321-5646

26. Lotus Development Corp.
55 Cambridge Parkway
Cambridge, MA 02142
800-554-5501

27. MECC
3490 Lexington Ave. North
St. Paul, MN 55126
800-228-3504

28. Mind Play
    100 Conifer Hill Drive
    Building 3, Suite 301
    Danvers, MA 01923
    800-221-7911

29. Mindscape
    3444 Dundee Road
    Northbrook, IL 60062
    800-221-9884

30. Scholastic, Inc.
    2931 E. McCarty Street
    P.O. Box 7502
    Jefferson City, MO 65102
    800-541-5513

31. Science Research Associates
    155 North Wacker Drive
    Chicago, IL 60606
    800-621-0476

32. Scott, Foresman
    1900 E. Lake Avenue
    Glenview, IL 60025
    312-729-3000

33. Sensible Software
    335 E. Big Beaver,
      Suite 207
    Troy, MI 48083
    810-528-1950

34. Software Garden
    Box 373
    Newton Highlands, MA 02161
    617-332-2240

35. Software Toolworks
    One Toolworks Plaza
    13557 Venture Blvd.
    Sherman Oaks, VA 91423
    818-907-6789

36. South-Western Publish. Co.
    5101 Madison Road
    Cincinnati, OH 45227
    800-543-7007

37. Sunburst Communications
    39 Washington Avenue
    Pleasantville, NY 10570-9971
    800-431-1934

38. Techbyte Inc.
    21 South Union Street
    Burlington, VT 05401
    800-361-4993

39. Tescor Inc.
    461 Carlisle Drive
    Herndon, VA 22070
    703-435-9501

40. Weekly Reader Software
    Optimum Resource Inc.
    10 Station Place
    Norfolk, CT 06058
    800-327-1473

41. Word Perfect Corp.
    329 N. State
    Orem, UT 84057
    800-321-4566

EVALUATING EDUCATIONAL SOFTWARE

What to Consider

Instructional Quality

    a. General—good length, appropriate directions or explanations, usefulness (better than another way), appropriateness of content—ethical—meets standards.

    b. Content—appropriate for level, current, accurate, free of errors, bias, and is relevant.

     c. Creativity—innovative, challenging, student empowering, and evaluative.

     d. Feedback—positive, relevant, timely, informative, correctly explains, gives variety of responses, uses bridging to other levels or sequences.

     e. Teacher friendly—easily used, can be changed to add or delete, can regulate number of problems, rate, percentage correct for mastery, and so on.

For more information see Appendix B, Power On—New Tools for Teaching and Learning—Congress of the U.S. Office of Technology Assessment, 1988.

Index